How to Organize
INCLUSIVE
EVENTS
and
CONFERENCES

ALEX D. KETCHUM

MICROCOSM PUBLISHING
PORTLAND, OR ● CLEVELAND, OH

How to Organize

Inclusive
Events *and*
Conferences

Alex D. Ketchum

Microcosm Publishing
Portland, OR | Cleveland, OH

HOW TO ORGANIZE INCLUSIVE EVENTS AND CONFERENCES
© Alex D. Ketchum, 2026

This edition © Microcosm Publishing, February 3, 2026
First Edition, 3000 copies
9781648415579
Ebook ISBN 9781648415272
This is Microcosm # 1006

Edited by Ivy Zeller
Designed by Joe Biel and Sarah Koch
For a catalog, write or visit:
Microcosm Publishing
2752 N Williams Ave.
Portland, OR 97227

All the news from the misfits in print at www.Microcosm.Pub/Newsletter
Get more copies of this book at www.Microcosm.Pub/InclusiveEvents
EU Safety Information: https://microcosmpublishing.com/gpsr

To join the ranks of high-class stores that feature Microcosm titles, talk to your rep: In the U.S. COMO (Atlantic), ABRAHAM (Midwest), BOB BARNETT (Texas, Oklahoma, Arkansas, Louisiana), IMPRINT (Pacific), TURNAROUND (UK), UTP/MANDA (Canada), NEWSOUTH (Australia/New Zealand), Observatoire (Africa, Europe), IPR (Middle East), APD (Asia), HarperCollins (India), and FAIRE in the gift trade.

Did you know that you can buy our books directly from us at sliding scale rates? Support a small, independent publisher and pay less than Amazon's price at www.Microcosm.Pub.

Global labor conditions are bad, and our roots in industrial Cleveland in the '70s and '80s made us appreciate the need to treat workers right. Therefore, our books are MADE IN THE USA.

Microcosm's workers and authors are paid solely from book sales. If you downloaded this book from some sketchy part of the Internet or picked up what appears to be a bootleg, please support our hardworking team by purchasing a copy directly from us and encouraging your communities to do the same. Paying for our books and zines helps us publish work that's far better than anything AI can come up with. Additionally, a 2025 MIT study revealed that AI inhibits humanity's critical thinking ability. Since critical thinking is one of our core values, we prohibit any use of our books to "train" generative artificial "intelligence" (AI) technologies, because seriously, WTF.

Library of Congress Control Number: 2025027784

MICROCOSM·PUBLISHING

Microcosm Publishing is Portland's most diversified publishing house and distributor with a focus on the colorful, authentic, and empowering. Our books and zines have put your power in your hands since 1996, equipping readers to make positive changes in their lives and in the world around them. Microcosm emphasizes skill-building, showing hidden histories, and fostering creativity through challenging conventional publishing wisdom with books and bookettes about DIY skills, food, bicycling, gender, self-care, and social justice. What was once a distro and record label started by Joe Biel in a drafty bedroom was determined to be *Publisher's Weekly's* fastest growing publisher of 2022 and has become among the oldest independent publishing houses in Portland, OR and Cleveland, OH. We are a politically moderate, centrist publisher in a world that has inched to the right for the past 80 years.

CONTENTS

Part 1: Foundations — 9

Introduction — 11
Defining Terms — 13
Initial Planning — 18

Part 2: Events — 27

Types of Events — 29
Size — 31
Location — 31
Timing — 44
Scheduling — 50
Organizing Alone or with a Team — 51
Money/Costs — 53
Speakers/Performers — 59
Language/Communication — 63
Publicity/Advertising — 68
Childcare — 75
Designated Areas — 77
Food/Drinks — 80
Tech/IT — 83
Factors You Need to Consider for Specific Event Types — 97

Part 3: Multiple Events Grouped Together: Conferences/Conventions 105

Types of Conferences   107
Types of Events at Conferences   109
Timeline for Organizing a Conference   114
Format/Flow of the Conference   128
Collaborative Events   130
Call for Papers/Presentations (CFP)   131
Your Team   142
Registration   150
Conference Website   152
Publicity/Advertising for Conferences   156
Conference Programs/Booklets ...and Getting Creative   157
SWAG and Merch   158
Lodging/Housing   159
Conference Check-In/Sign-In/Welcome Table   160
End-of-Day Reflection   163
Publications   163
Wrapping Up   166

Part 4: Organizer Needs 171

In Your Bag   173
Self-Care   174
Navigating Success and Failure   178
When to Stop: Navigating Endings   182
Conclusion and Acknowledgments   185
Additional Resources   187
About the Author   190

PART 1: FOUNDATIONS

INTRODUCTION

*H*ave you ever wanted to organize a public event? Do you dream of hosting a battle of the bands, film screenings, concerts, poetry readings, art shows, teach-ins, lectures, seed exchanges, zine workshops, and panels? What about a conference? Maybe you already have experience doing this work but you have noticed that inequities from the society-at-large are replicated at your events, despite best intentions.

The goal of this book is to provide event and conference organizers of all levels with the tools to make their events accessible, sustainable, and rooted in social justice principles. Whether you are new to organizing or highly experienced, this book will provide frameworks and practical tips to create inclusive events. No matter the kind of event or conference you are interested in organizing, whether large or small, online, in-person, hybrid, synchronous, or asynchronous, this book includes what you need to know. From the smallest details (such as what to have in your bag on the day of the gathering) to large topics (such as choosing a location, selecting presenters, funding, designing publicity materials, working with community partners, etc.)

This book draws on my experience organizing hundreds of public events, including:

- 100+ events for Disrupting Disruptions: The Feminist and Accessible Publishing, Communications, and Tech Hybrid Speaker and Workshop Series

- several conferences, including:

○ Queer Food Conference (Boston and Montréal)

○ Food, Feminism, and Fermentation Conference

○ *Circuits de consommation*, a food, feminism, and technology conference

• Multiple Feminist Research Colloquiums.

I have also organized concerts, book launches, pumpkin festivals, sports tournaments, dances, parties, potlucks, podcasting workshops, film screenings, rallies, marches, and parades.

As both an organizer and attendee, I have paid attention to what worked, what did not work, and what could be improved. I will also share insights from other event organizers, disability justice activists, feminist educators, and queer designers.

How we do the work is the work. In this book, I hope to help you organize events and conferences that reflect the ethos that inspired your event in the first place. We will explore how decisions over signage, outreach, website design, food, pricing, venue, technology, and so much more can foreground queer, feminist, accessible, socially just, and inclusive principles. This book will help you host an event or conference in which everyone who takes part feels included, supported, and valued!

This book begins in Part 1 by exploring the foundations of inclusive event and conference organizing. Part 2 focuses on event organizing. Much of the content in Part 2 informs Part 3, which focuses specifically on conference planning. Part 4 focuses on your needs as an organizer.

One other note: Part 2, the section on events, can inform your conference organizing decisions . . . because conferences are, in essence, a series of smaller events, grouped together.

While each section of the book builds on the next, I encourage you to flip to different sections as they are most useful for you. Templates for your event and conference organizing are distributed throughout the book. If your phone has word detection capabilities, you can turn your camera app on and select the text so you can use the templates more readily. Adjust them to your needs.

Finally, although I may mention certain applications and software, technology is ever-evolving. I encourage you to focus more on the technological capabilities of any tool (whether paper, email, computer software, or a phone app) and how they can serve the values of your conference rather than the exact software I discuss.

This book contains information that will help guide your decisions to ensure that your event is inclusive and reflects your goals and values.

Let's get organizing!

DEFINING TERMS

*A*s this book aims to encourage accessible design and organization, it is important to define the terminology used in it. Language has the ability to connect or create barriers. While the sections on interpreters, CART captioning, and publicity will discuss language and inclusion in more detail, below are definitions of terms that will appear throughout this book.

Accessibility and Design Justice

When we talk about accessibility, what do we mean? Do we mean that the event is wheelchair-friendly? Do we mean that there is a sign language interpreter? Is there a translator for people who do not speak the primary language at the event? Is there a lactation room for parents? Is there an all-gender bathroom? What about the cost of tickets?

Design justice is a framework that aims to center the voices of people who are normally marginalized and directly impacted by the outcomes of the design process (including event and conference organizing). Prioritizing accessibility from a design justice perspective, not only benefits individuals with visible or known physical, psychological, or cognitive disabilities, but works to ensure that all participants are able to fully engage in the program:

- participants with disabilities and/or chronic health conditions;
- people of all ages and body types;
- individuals across the gender spectrum and of all sexual orientations;
- and folks from all class, racial, and ethnic backgrounds.

Rather than focus on making "accommodations," which creates a burden for the individual participant and acts as a retroactive patch to overcome barriers in an environment or system, accessibility from a design justice standpoint means that you will design your event to be inclusive from the start. The goal is that the event will not require adaptation or modification to remove barriers to participation, while being cognizant of conflicting or competing access needs.

But what happens when access needs conflict or compete with each other? For example, one or more participants may require low lighting because bright lights can trigger sensory overload or migraines. And at the same event, someone might need brighter lighting in order to see an interpreter or read documents.

While all access needs are valid, sometimes not all access needs can be provided simultaneously. You want to create an environment where participants feel safe and comfortable to ask for accommodations. When you share information about your event, it is useful to provide information about what accessibility features are already in place. This practice allows individuals to make choices about whether they feel comfortable attending and can facilitate participants getting in touch about their own access needs and what provisions can be made. To learn more, check out the awesome work by the Design Justice Network (designjustice. org/read-the-principles)!

What does design justice mean for you as an event organizer? This book will help you consider accessibility throughout the entire process of planning and hosting an event. These principles will also guide how you promote and disseminate information about and from your event.

Feminism and Social Justice

There are many kinds of feminism, including but not limited to Liberal, Marxist, Socialist, Radical, Anarchist, Eco, Decolonial, Anticolonial, Indigenous, and Black Feminisms. There are debates and disagreements between feminists involved in these separate groups and within the groups themselves. These labels, furthermore, do not encompass all approaches to feminism. Each form of feminism has offered and continues to bring different strategies to tackle social injustice.

I am not interested in imposing a single prescriptive definition of feminism when discussing inclusive event organizing. For me, feminism in the broadest sense is about the social, political, and economic equity of all sexes and genders. Feminism, as defined in this book, seeks to create a socially just world and combat the forces of sexism, heterosexism, transphobia, racism, classism, ableism, and colonialism. Feminist and anti-racist writing, activism, research, and art practices deeply influence my approach and exposure to social justice and disability rights movements. Social justice, feminist, and disability rights activism interweave to inform the ways we create inclusive events.

Sustainability

Sustainability is key to accessible event organizing in two senses: environmental activism and as part of ethics of care.

Environmentalism and sustainability must be part of our discussion around inclusive organizing as pollution, climate change, and ecological degradation disproportionately affect the most marginalized members of our communities. Waste and dump sites are zoned near communities of color. Toxic oil refineries are placed next to or on Indigenous lands. Furthermore, disabled people face particular challenges during the climate crisis and may experience reduced access to healthcare services, food, water, and accessible infrastructure. For example, emergency shelters and infrastructure often lack proper accessibility, making evacuation or finding safe shelter more challenging, and power outages can threaten people who rely on electricity for essential medical devices. Our events cannot be truly inclusive if they contribute to ecological degradation. This handbook will help you consider the environmental impact of your event.

Sustainability, as a framework, also addresses the ability for something to be maintained at a certain rate or level. Let us consider an ethics of care in which the material conditions of the organizer, presenter/performer, and audience/participant/attendee are taken into account:

- Can you organize events in a manner that is sustainable to your wellbeing and health as the host?
- How can you make sure that the needs of the performers or presenters are met?
- What is the role of compensation in ensuring the sustainability of your event?

With care and social justice at the center of your organizing work, your events can bolster connection to others and build communities. Toward that end, this book will help you consider the ways in which your event or conference sustains you and your participants.

Other Terms

There are other terms that appear throughout the book that can be used within event organizing.

Honorarium: An honorarium is usually a one-time payment intended to compensate an individual for a service rendered. Rather than an hourly rate, honorariums are a lump sum payment, determined before the start of the event.

CFP: The acronym CFP stands for "call for papers" and/or "call for proposals." A CFP invites participants to submit proposals for talks, workshops, panels, or papers in advance of conferences and publications. This term is often used in relation to conferences.

SWAG: This acronym stands for "Stuff We All Get" or "Souvenirs, Wearables, and Gifts." These materials can be distributed to event participants. Examples include t-shirts, hats, pens, tote bags, water bottles, and other items that often have the event name included on them.

INITIAL PLANNING

*O*ne of the most exciting stages of event and conference organizing is the initial period when you can imagine, hope, and dream. The below sections on brainstorming are bolstered by the materials throughout this book. Return to these brainstorming exercises after reading through the book to see if you can amend any of your plans to make them even more inclusive.

Brainstorming Round 1: What Kind of Event Do You Want to Create?

First things first, what kind of event are you organizing? A concert? A rally? A poetry reading? A teach-in? A lecture? A panel? A fire-side chat? A discussion roundtable? An art show? A live taping? A book reading? A coffeehouse open mic? A workshop? A performance? A conference?

There are so many forms public events can take. For more ideas, see "Types of Events" in Part 2.

It can be helpful to draw or write out your ideas of how you envision your event happening. In doing so, you can get a sense of what kind of equipment and resources you will require. This process can also help you figure out a schedule.

I suggest a multi-step process for brainstorming. In your initial brainstorming, it is useful to think about the big 5 questions: who, what, where, when, and how.

Who: Who is your intended audience? Who is your presenter/performer/entertainment? How many people do you want to/expect to come? Who will be organizing the event; will it be you or a team of people?

What: What type of event is this? What do you want to happen? What kind of format will the event follow? What amenities will you provide at the event? What kind of equipment will you need? What materials are necessary?

When: What date will the event take place? Is it one day? Several days? Is it recurring? Is it part of a series? What time of day will it take place?

Where: Where is the event going to take place? Will it take place in cyberspace? Will it be hybrid? Will you have to rent a venue? Is the venue accessible only by stairs? How much do you have to pay to use the space?

Why: Why are you hosting this event? Why is an event like this necessary?

How: How will you fund the event? How will you advertise? How will you ensure that your event aligns with your values? How will you define the success of your event? How will diversity of experience and identity be interwoven into the event?

The answers to these questions can have a large impact on the inclusivity of your event.

Round 2 of Brainstorming
After the first round of brainstorming, it will be useful to start to be more specific about the details of your event or conference

What is the . . .
- theme/topic of the event or conference?
- name or title of the event or conference?
- type of event (a workshop, festival, etc.)?
- estimated number of participants?
- estimated amount of speakers/presenters performers?
- estimated number of events (workshops, panels, keynotes, etc.)?

- length of the event (one hour, one day, several days, etc.)?
- start time of the event? end time?
- date of your event? Your ideal schedule?
- venue? location?
- format? online? in person? hybrid?

Other questions to consider . . .
General:

- Do you need any special licensing such as liquor permits if you intend to serve alcohol or a permit to host a march or event on public lands? Towns and cities often have information about required permits on their websites.
- If you have gone to other similar events, what did you like? How can you incorporate these components into your event?
- If you have gone to other similar events, what did you not like? How can you avoid these issues?
- Will you provide honorariums for speakers, workshop leaders, and performers? If so, how much? Cash, checks, e-payment? Who is going to handle the payment paperwork? How long will payment take? Will you pay people before or after the conference? Will you pay in installments?

Format of Multi-Event Events:

If you are hosting a conference, festival, convention, or other event with several component events included, what kinds of events will you include? How long will these events be? If events are different lengths, how will this impact scheduling if you have multiple streams happening simultaneously?

Partnered Events/Collaborations:

- Are you organizing every event or will you partner with other folks or organizations to host partner events?

- Will collaborator-organized events happen during the core schedule of the main event or conference or will collaborator-organized events occur after hours/ outside of conference hours?

- Do collaborator-organized events have separate registration or ticketing?

- How will you decide which folks to partner with? What values do you want to align with? Are you comfortable with corporate sponsorship?

Funding:

- What upfront costs do you have? Do you have to make a down payment on the location? What about website design, domain names, or hosting? Are you paying for any advertising?

- What are your estimated total costs including location, rental of tables, chairs, tech, catering costs, and honorariums for keynote speakers?

- Will you apply for grants?

- When are the grants due and what do they require?

- Will you seek sponsors? How will you decide what kinds of sponsors align with your values?

- Will you have tickets? Will they be sold on a sliding scale? How will you charge for tickets?

- Will the event be free?

Volunteers/Crew:

- How many folks do you need to work the event? What is the minimum number? What is the ideal?

- Will people be paid? If not, will they be compensated in other ways (t-shirts, food, comped entrance fees, school credit, something else)?

- How long will shifts be for longer events?

- Will you have a practice run-through in advance of the event?

- How will you communicate with the crew?

Tech Needs:

- What kind of tech do you need?

- Microphones or voice amplifiers?

- Speakers?

- Cables or extension cords?

- Projectors?

- Computers? Will presenters bring their own?

- Dongles to connect to projectors?

- Musical instruments?

- Do participants need wifi or an internet connection? Is there a wifi code? Is it publicly available? If not, how will you distribute it?

- If there is an artistic installation: What special tech needs do the artists or performers have? How will you collect this information in advance?

Food:

- Are you going to provide food?

- Will you hire caterers?

- What types of foods will you offer and how will you make sure to provide food for people with allergies and different kinds of diets (vegetarian, vegan, halal, kosher, etc.)?

- How will you collect information about the dietary restrictions of participants in advance? If your event has registration, will this information be collected as part of the registration form?

- Will food be free? Included with certain kinds of tickets? Or available for purchase?

- Will you work with vendors such as food trucks and coffee carts?

- If there is cooking on site, what special tools do the cooks need?

- Do caterers need any special equipment?

- If there is not running water, how will you make sure to have enough potable water?

- Will you provide reusable plates, bowls, and cutlery, or disposable or compostable ones? Will you wash dishware?

Music:

- Will you play music? If so, what?

- Will there be speakers and/or a sound system on site? Do you need to rent one?

- Will you hire musicians?

- Will you monitor sound levels so that they are in a safe range (below 85 dB and ideally below 70 dB)?

Decorations:
- Will there be decorations?

- What is your budget for decorations?

- How far in advance of the event can you decorate?

- Have you made sure that the decorations will not impede accessibility within the space?

Publicity and Registration:
- How will you publicize your event?

- Will you create social media posts for your event? What social media platforms will you use? What accounts will you use? Will you create social media accounts specifically for your event, especially if it is part of a recurring series or a conference? Will you use alt text?

- Will you print physical flyers? Will you pay for advertisements? Will you share information on listservs?

- Do you have other publicity strategies? Will you get creative? Will you hire a skywriter? Send mailers? What are the environmental and financial costs of these strategies?

- What languages will you use on these publicity materials?

- Will you create a logo or coherent design aesthetic for your publicity?

- Will you have participants register in advance? If so, how will you handle registration? Will you use a platform?

- Can people show up without registering in advance?

Cleanup:

- Do you have crew members assigned to this task?

- Will you have compost and recycling? Is this something already available at the venue or will you have to arrange this yourself? Do you have the supplies necessary?

In the following pages, you will find more information to help you answer these questions.

PART 2: EVENTS

*I*f you are reading this book to learn about conference organizing specifically, this section on events in general can inform your decisions: because conferences, at their heart, are a series of smaller events, grouped together. Regardless of event type, the following pages include a wealth of information to help you with every step of organizing.

TYPES OF EVENTS

*W*hat even is an *event*? In the most basic sense, events are about bringing people together. There are so many types of events and each one has unique characteristics that can impact accessibility. Below is a list of some event types.

Are you thinking of hosting a . . .

- literary/book/publishing event?

  - examples: a zine fair, a literary festival, a book launch, a reading, a poetry slam, a small press conference, or a comics convention

- music, theater, or comedy event?

  - examples: a concert, a battle of the bands, a performance, a master class, a comedy showcase, a stand-up or improv show, a fire-side chat with a composer, a live taping, or a music festival

- food-based event?

  - examples: a food festival, a food studies conference, a potluck, a community pancake breakfast, a pop-up, a seed workshop, a pumpkin or spring flower festival on a farm, a kitchen takeover, a seedling exchange, a lecture on urban agriculture, a garden party, a beer or wine tasting, a baking class, or a cooking demo

- film, visual arts, or dance event?

- examples: an outdoor film screening, a film festival, a bike-powered animated shorts showcase, a vernissage, an exhibition opening, a guided tour, a curator talk, a dance performance, or a dance party

- political event?

  - examples: a rally, a march, a parade, a demonstration, or a protest

- sports event?

  - examples: roller derby matches, a bike repair workshop, a lacrosse tournament, a holiday 5k run, a critical mass bike ride, a city triathlon, a cross country ski loppet, or an ice skating show

- sustainability-focused event?

  - examples: a beach cleanup, a river walk, or a free yoga class in the park

- recurring event?

  - examples: a lecture or speaker series, a craft or knitting circle, or a weekly line dance party

While all of these events have unique features, key organizing choices can make them more inclusive, welcoming, and sustainable. There are several factors to consider when planning any kind of event or conference, including size, location, timing, scheduling, money/cost, invited speakers and performers, language/communication, whether you will organize alone or with a team, money/costs, speakers/performers, language/communication, publicity/advertising, childcare, designated areas, food/drinks, and tech/IT.

SIZE

*E*vents and conferences can range widely in size. The scale of your event and conference will impact all other decisions. Finding a venue for 20 people is very different for 200 (or 2000!) people. Providing food and SWAG for 50 people is a different undertaking than for 5000. Your decisions over size will greatly impact later choices about venue, format, cost, applications for presenters, and collaborators.

Several factors can help you decide the size of your event including location, how niche your topic is, the amount of time you can dedicate to organizing the event, and the budget. If your event is for an organization that has 70 members that all would need to attend, then you already know your general size. If you need or want to host your event at a specific location that has an occupancy capacity of 50 people, then the decision is made for you (though you can likely accept 5-8% more people than the capacity due to last minute cancellations and not everyone arriving at the same time). However, physical space is not the only mitigating factor if you have virtual or hybrid components.

If this is your first time organizing an event or conference, consider starting with a smaller event of 50 people or fewer. The larger the event, the more components you will have to manage. You can always organize a larger event or conference in the future.

LOCATION

*Y*ou will need to decide whether your event will happen in-person, in cyberspace, or in a combination of the two. The choice of in-person versus digital/virtual events influences your ability to reach different communities and audiences. While a digital event means that someone across the planet can participate, not everyone has computers, phones, or access to the internet (or a strong and stable wifi connection). If you hope to congregate folks from your local community, it is likely that you will choose to hold an in-person event. Consider disseminating materials related to the event, such as recordings or publications, so that individuals who couldn't attend otherwise can still be involved.

Your choices around location will impact for whom the event is accessible. In-person events mean that either people have to live locally or travel, which may not be financially accessible for everyone. People who are unable to leave their home due to caregiving responsibilities or different disabilities will not be able to participate. Virtual events require access to a strong internet connection, a technological device, and often a quiet, private space for participation. Hybrid events can expand participation, mitigating some of the barriers of virtual or in-person only events, but are more difficult to organize—and not every event translates into a hybrid format well.

In this section, we'll cover these and other factors related to event location.

Virtual vs. In-Person

Virtual

Virtual events can enable people from around the world to connect synchronously or asynchronously (people can watch or listen after the recording). By going virtual, the financial and environmental cost of travel to in-person events can be reduced. However, it is important to remember that virtual events still have a material impact through electricity, internet infrastructure, and the mining of materials for our computers and devices. While digital tools expand accessibility in some senses, it is important to note that marginalized communities are more likely to face online harassment including trolling and doxxing. Security breaches during virtual conferences and events have resulted in "zoombombings"—a phenomenon in which people use the platform to harass the presenter or participants. Additionally, if the nature of your event is particularly political, you will want to consider the cybersecurity of your event. Online spaces can be violent spaces.

Video Chat / Webinar Services
Video chat and webinar services can be useful for events in which you want the audience to be able to speak and ask questions. Some software allows you to record the video chat and share the footage after the conference.

During 2020 and subsequent COVID-19 pandemic years, many folks became more familiar with video chat services such as Zoom, Google Meet, and Microsoft Teams. Another option is Jitsi, a free and open source video conferencing tool (jitsi.org). For many of these services, use is free up to a specified number of users or for a certain amount of time. Services such as Zoom also provide webinar options, which allow a greater control over security features. If you are running multiple events simultaneously during your conference, you will need to enable several meetings or webinars at once and make all of these links available to the conference participants so they can pop into the room or webinar of their choice.

Features on these platforms continue to change. You can often enable features for language interpretation including sign language and CART captioning. If you are not working with a human CART captioner, make sure to enable auto-captions on the platform you use. Captions can be useful to many people: those who are Deaf, hard of hearing, are participating in a second language, etc.

If you are sharing a live musical performance via Zoom, use the strongest wifi available, leave the "automatically adjust microphone volume" box unchecked so that the software doesn't attempt to auto-adjust sound levels based on the preset for speaking voices, and make sure everyone else is on mute. Encourage participants to lower their bandwidth or data usage by turning off their HD video and for people to only share their screens for as long as necessary.

With all that in mind, remember that no solution is perfect. Software is ever-changing. It is important to consider cost, encryption, security, simplicity of the user interface, number of users allowed, and the ability to record.

Live Streaming

You can choose to livestream an event that is happening in-person with many people physically present or you can livestream a single speaker or a group call. Popular live stream platforms include: YouTube (owned by Google), Facebook Live (owned by Meta), Twitch (owned by Amazon), and Instagram Stories (owned by Meta). The benefit with these platforms is that all you need is a smartphone (or computer) and a free account. Most of these platforms also include a space where audiences can ask questions or post comments in real time. Platforms like YouTube and Vimeo also make it easy to save the video so that it is available after the event ends so that people can watch the event at a later time, making the event even more accessible. YouTube also auto-generates closed captioning for videos.

Hybrid

When done well, hybrid events enable people to gather in-person while creating the opportunity for others to participate from afar. When done poorly, in-person and virtual participants all leave the event feeling dissatisfied. Therefore, hybrid events require the most advanced preparation and ongoing moderation of the three options.

Hybrid events are most successful when organizers allocate sufficient staffing for the virtual rooms and virtual participants. More information (including a step-by-step setup) is available in the tech section, but plan to have one person in charge of monitoring the virtual livestream and comments per workshop, panel, roundtable, or talk. Having dedicated crew members who can respond to technical difficulties and guide presenters and participants ensures a smoother experience for everyone involved. Proper staffing means that care for all participants can be centered, whether folks are in-person or virtual.

Factors to Consider for In-Person Events (or the In-Person Components of Hybrid Events)

When it comes to booking physical spaces or venues for your conference, there are a lot of things to consider if you want your event to be inclusive. Cost of renting or using a space can impact whether or not you charge for the event and this in turn can impact who can attend. The availability of the space may affect the date/timing of the event. If you decide to have an event outdoors, you might have to take rental costs of port-o-potties, electrical connections, and table rentals into consideration. The structure of the space can also impact accessibility and the kinds of programming you can offer.

Below are suggestions to consider when choosing a space for your event.

- Can the room only be entered by climbing stairs or a steep hill? Stairs mean that people with reduced mobility and wheelchair users will not be able to attend. If there are elevators, are they wide enough for wheelchairs and scooters?

- Are the door frames of the venue wide enough for a wheelchair or scooter to pass through? 32 inches or 82 cm (preferably wider)? Is there a bump over the threshold? Even a 1 inch or 2.5 cm bump can pose an issue for wheelchair users. Threshold ramps can mitigate this problem.

- Have you allocated space for service animals? Is there access to the outdoors for service dogs?

- If doors are closed, do the doors have lever handles and/or are they equipped with an automatic opener? If not, will you have someone at the entrance to welcome people into the room?

- Is there a public transit option for people to travel to the event? Public transport is a class and environmental issue. (If you're in a major metropolitan area, Google added wheelchair accessible routes to Google Maps on both desktop and mobile.)

- Are there designated parking spots near the entrance for people with disabilities?

- Is there a barrier-free path for people to travel from the parking lot or drop-off area to the venue entrance?

- If you are hosting the event in a place with snow or ice, will the paths be cleared?

- If the event is being held at an outdoor site, will the surface be accessible for persons using wheelchairs and scooters?

- If the main entrance is not accessible, is there a sign clearly visible at the front of the building that indicates the location of an accessible entrance? Make sure to circulate information about accessibility features in advance of the event as well (the conference website is a great place for this information).

- Is there a wheelchair accessible washroom/bathroom? Are the sinks reachable from a wheelchair?

- Is there an all-gender washroom/bathroom? If the venue does not have a single-use washroom or all gender washrooms, are you able to temporarily change the bathroom signs for the event? The ability to access a washroom is a basic human right. A lack of all-gender washrooms can make your event non-inclusive for trans and non-binary individuals.

- Is there a space for people who are nursing? Is there an electrical outlet for breast/chest pumps?

- Will you be able to provide chairs for people who may need to sit? Chair availability can be particularly important for, but not limited to, people with various disabilities, the elderly, and pregnant individuals.

- Can you rearrange chairs/ move chairs so that wheelchair users can have a seat at the table? Near the stage? Is it possible to arrange sitting in circles, so that people who are hard of hearing can see people's faces?

- Will your conference take place in one room? Or multiple? How far is the distance between these spaces? Does your schedule have enough time to accommodate movement between these spaces?

- How will you ensure people with a low-stimuli threshold will be able to find a quieter space?

- Are you able to control the lighting? Fluorescent lighting can cause headaches, which make it difficult to participate.

- Can you guarantee a scent-free environment, including in the washrooms? Due to scent sensitivities, which can cause nausea and headaches, ask participants in advance to refrain from using strong perfumes and soaps.

- If hosting the conference outdoors, do you need to rent toilets? Do you have the electricity you need? What about rain? Will you rent a tent? Will you need to rent tables and chairs?

- If you are hosting a multi-day conference, is there lodging nearby? Are you able to offer lodging at a discounted cost or at a sliding scale?

It will also be important to consider your technological needs for the conference. While the tech section will discuss this more, some questions to consider are as follows:

- Do rooms already have projectors? Can you rent or bring in your own projectors?

- What about sound systems? Microphones?

- Are there enough outlets? Does the venue charge extra for electricity use?

- Is there wifi? How can people access it?

Booking Rooms/Spaces/Venues/Locations
Your budget will also influence your choice of venue.

When renting a venue, it is important to check:

- the cost per hour (and to account for setup and take-down times)

- what equipment is provided (chairs, tables, sound equipment, etc.)

- what limitations there are regarding what you can do in the venue (catering, noise limits, security, etc.)

- if you are responsible for cleaning the space and bathrooms

- if there is no all-gender washroom/bathroom on site, whether or not you can change the signs for the day (even by putting a piece of paper over the permanent sign)

- if you need a permit to gather there

- if you need a permit to to serve alcohol

Free or Low Cost Options

Using free or low cost spaces is my preference as it means that the event budget (which sometimes is zero dollars) is not eaten up by the space rental. Depending on the community you are trying to reach with your event, these options may encourage or dissuade participation. Not everyone feels comfortable going to a university campus, a community center, or an event in a church basement, even though these may be low cost options.

Libraries: Libraries offer more than books! Your local library may have a room for gatherings, may have maker-spaces, and more. Check out what kinds of resources are available. Even if the library isn't the right venue for your event, you might be able to borrow audio visual (AV) equipment or other necessary materials there.

University or College Campuses/Schools: If you are a student or faculty member, it is usually possible to rent spaces on campus for free or low cost (especially if you are part of a student group, club, or organization). If you aren't a student or faculty member, can you collaborate with a student or faculty member for your event to get access to this free space? From classrooms to concert halls, universities and colleges offer a wide variety of options. Booking through the events office of a university might lead to higher costs than working with individuals you might know at a university who can book spaces for free or low cost through their department. Elementary, middle, and high schools might be options for you too.

Community Centers: "Community center" is a broad term that can refer to a wide range of resources and spaces available. They are typically public or semi-public locations where members of a community tend to gather for group activities, social support, public information, and other more. They may sometimes be open for use by the whole community or only for a specialized group within the greater community.

Religious Organizations: Some religious groups will rent out their spaces, particularly basements, even to non-community members. These spaces tend to be available at low or no cost. The choice to meet in the basement of a church, temple, mosque, or synagogue may deter participation from potential attendees, as well as potentially create obstacles to accessibility.

Local Music and Arts Venues: Depending on the venue, there can be a wide range of fees. Your city or town might have a cafe, restaurant, pub, bar, or gallery that offers free or low cost space or has sliding scales for events. Businesses that are explicit about their feminist, social justice, or anarchist politics tend to have more affordable options.

Public Parks: While public parks may have rules about the size of the gathering or time of day, as well as requiring permits, many public parks have bathrooms, running water, and some kind of structure. Using these facilities can be free or low cost.

On the Land: Want to host an outdoor event? You will likely need to also rent a tent for rain or to block direct sunlight. You might need to rent toilets, bring extension cords for electricity (or be off the grid), and don't forget: water! Therefore, due to those rental costs, hosting an event outdoors is not necessarily cheaper than using an indoor venue.

Your Own Home or Backyard: For a smaller public event, it might be possible to organize an event in your living space. You will need to check with the people you live with if they are comfortable with this decision. Be respectful of your neighbors, especially regarding noise levels. If your aim is an inclusive public event, people may not feel comfortable entering a private residence and it is also probably less likely that your home will be accessible for people with mobility disabilities.

Not Low Cost—Hotels and Conference/Convention Centers: Especially if you are hosting a conference, convention, or festival with thousands of people, you might consider hosting your event in a hotel or a conference/convention center. The benefit of using these spaces is that the facility is used to hosting these kinds of events. The downside is that the costs can be exorbitant and might mean you have to charge over $100 per participant. You might have to book these spaces more than one year in advance. Some hotels also offer packages which include discounted hotel rooms for people traveling from out of town.

General Tip

Talk to other event organizers from your town to get local tips and tricks. Also if you are going to pay to use a space, it is great if your dollars can support a business or organization that you respect.

Colonial Context of Space and Land Acknowledgements

Acknowledging the history of unceded territories on which your conference is taking place, as well as the history of the space, is an important practice. Land or territory acknowledgements occur at the beginning of public events. They are often concise and follow a format like, "I want to acknowledge that we are on the traditional territory of [nation names]," though they can be more comprehensive. It is important that if you are giving the acknowledgement, you know how to properly pronounce the name of the nation or community. It is even better if you can learn the name of the nation or community in its original language. Ideally a member of that community will give the opening address. You need to financially compensate this person and provide an honorarium gift.

The violence of the colonization of North America is not relegated to the past. The ongoing impacts of colonization shape our present society. Land acknowledgements raise awareness about Indigenous presence and land rights. They encourage settlers to recognize the history and political reality of the United States and Canada, which is often omitted from school curriculum.

Native Land Digital (native-land.ca) has created an invaluable resource, including a map that indicates Indigenous territories, languages, and treaties, a teacher's guide, and a list of further resources to help people understand the histories of the lands that we live and work on.

Even if your event is virtual only, everything we do is tied to the land. We must always be mindful of the lands that the servers enabling our virtual events are on. Indigenous communities are disproportionately impacted by the mining practices used for the materials that are used to build our computers and digital infrastructure.

There is some critique that land acknowledgements are token gestures, especially when the people doing them and the audience hearing them do not think about the steps beyond acknowledging the territory where the event is taking place. How can we have reconciliation if we don't have justice?

In response, Chelsea Vowel, a Métis writer and scholar from the Plains Cree speaking community of Lac Ste. Anne, Alberta, writes the following in "Beyond Territorial Acknowledgements," a resource at Apihtawikosisan.com, her website: "If we think of territorial acknowledgments as sites of potential disruption, they can be transformative acts that to some extent undo Indigenous erasure. I believe this is true as long as these acknowledgments discomfit both those speaking and hearing the words. The fact of Indigenous presence should force non-Indigenous peoples to confront their own place on these lands."

Land acknowledgements are merely a starting place. They do not replace the necessary work of reconciliation. The Truth and Reconciliation Commission of Canada's 94 calls to action (ehprnh2mwo3.exactdn.com/wp-content/uploads/2021/01/Calls_to_Action_English2.pdf) provide a framework for this work.

You might also be able to integrate material support for local Indigenous communities as part of your event. Is it possible to donate part of the proceeds from the event towards a local Indigenous community organization? Or share information about and links to local community organizations?

Acknowledging Other Forms of Violence Related to the Space of the Event

The United States and Canada built their nations through the practice of enslaving Black and Indigenous peoples. The violent legacy of slavery continues across society, ranging from racialized economic disparity, high rates of incarceration of people of color, and lower life expectancies and less access to medical care for communities of color. I hold many events and conferences at McGill University. The founder of McGill University, James McGill, was an enslaver and he economically benefited through his choice to enslave others. With this money, McGill University was founded. I acknowledge this fact at the start of events I host on campus, as the histories of violence within our institutions continue to influence and impact the kinds of conversations that are had.

Wherever your event ends up occurring, I encourage you to think critically about the role of space in the conferences that you organize.

TIMING

*W*ill your conference be synchronous, asynchronous, or synchronous with recordings? Your decision will impact who, how, and when people will be able to engage with the event.

Synchronous

A synchronous conference is ephemeral. People either go to an event or miss it. Many conferences already operate in this way. Attendees select which panels, workshops, and events to attend and if they do not go during the scheduled time, they will miss it. Benefits include people feeling motivated to go to the event knowing it will be their only opportunity. Presenters might feel more inclined to experiment with ideas or be spontaneous. However, synchronous-only events limit who can participate.

Asynchronous

Asynchronous events can take many forms. Presenters might pre-record presentations and share them on a speakers series webpage, a conference website, or a YouTube channel. Alternative asynchronous conferences might consist of collecting and distributing materials such as zines to all participants. The first asynchronous conference I ever attended was Climate Change: A View from the Humanities, held in 2016. The organizers sought to create a close-to-carbon-neutral conference by discouraging travel. Participants pre-recorded video presentations and attendees asked questions in a comment section. While some participants were able to make connections, the experience served as a reminder that even if components of the conference are asynchronous, it can be useful to include synchronous events where participants are encouraged to interact.

Asynchronous conferences can be useful forums for knowledge sharing, but unless they include some synchronous components, such as in-person, virtual, or hybrid social hours, these events are less useful for networking, community building, and socializing. Furthermore, as participants might know that they can access materials at any time, they might actually continue to procrastinate interacting with video recordings or printed documents. If you do organize an asynchronous conference, consider having a chat function or another way that participants can ask presenters questions.

Platforms that facilitate virtual interactions might be useful for your conference. For example, Gather, previously known as Gather Town, is an interactive virtual space that seeks to simulate real-life, in-person interactions. With an 8-bit pixelated video game aesthetic and fairly intuitive online video and chat features, Gather enables users to move through online spaces using their arrow keys for keyboard controls. Users create an avatar who can move in and out of interactions and conversations with other participants they encounter and explore galleries of digital objects, including videos and sound files. Other similar platforms include Kumospace, Teemyco, and HyHyve, all with different features and pricing.

To Record or Not Record?
Many folks love the idea of recording events. On the one hand,

recordings can make materials accessible to a larger range of folks, can serve as an important record of what occurred during the event, and can enable participants to attend panels or other conference events that were scheduled concurrently. However, recordings can add another layer of complexity. While many webinar and online meeting platforms enable recordings to either the cloud or desktop with a click of a button, there are other technical challenges. You will need to determine where these recordings will be stored. Consider the following questions:

- Who will be allowed to access the recordings?

- How will they have access?

- Will you upload everything to a video sharing platform such as YouTube or Vimeo?

- Who will transfer the videos to that platform?

- How will you receive consent from the presenters for the video recordings?

- Will you provide a form presenters must fill out?

- What about the participants—especially in participatory events such as workshops in which many folks might appear in the recording?

- Will you have a blanket statement that by participating in the event a person is consenting to be recorded?

- How long will the recordings be made available?

- After that period of availability ends, will the recordings be stored anywhere or deleted?

- Do you have a plan for long-term maintenance of the video recording files?

Furthermore, people might feel more guarded and less willing to experiment with ideas knowing they are recorded. If you have included CART captioners or language interpreters as part of your event, fees are often higher if the event is recorded so you will need to adjust your budget to account for the recording fee. Participants might be less likely to participate in events synchronously if they think they will watch the recording later (which they may or may not do) and this can impact the discussion and participation during the synchronous event. If the event includes third party materials, such as music from someone not involved in the performance or event, you might not be legally allowed to share the recording publicly.

It is important that you discuss recording with any presenters in advance of the event so that the presenters can provide informed consent rather than feel pressured moments before the event starts. If you are recording an event, make sure that participants are informed of how or if their presence will be recorded.

Technical Tips
The sound quality of a recording will be improved if the speaker(s) uses a microphone.

If you do decide to record your conference events and have hired CART captioners, you will want that set of captions included in the video rather than the auto-generated captions from services such as YouTube. The following instructions are specific to Zoom but will be similar on other platforms. After the conference event ends (either a single event or maybe you have had the same Zoom meeting going for eight hours), you will need to download the recording and the transcripts if prompted to do so. Download the recording package from the Zoom website once Zoom has finished processing the recording.

During this process, you will need to clean the CART generated transcript. I am grateful to Kit Chokly for creating a template for cleaning the transcript so it is useful on video services such YouTube. Thanks, Kit, for giving us permission to share!

Step 1: Download the recording.

- When the event ends, download the transcripts if prompted to do so.

- Download the recording package from the Zoom website once Zoom has finished processing the recording.

Step 2: Clean the transcript.

- Create a new Google Doc and copy/paste in the contents of the .vtt captions file

- Title the doc "[EVENT or PRESENTER NAME] Transcript"

- Go Edit > Find & Replace

- Ensure the that "Use regular expressions" box is checked

- Use the following instructions, copying and pasting the content (including any leading or trailing spaces) within the quotes.

- NOTE: If something weird happens in this process, you can always go Edit > Undo and try again.

  ○ Find: "[0-9][0-9]:"

  ○ Click: "Replace all"

- Repeat:

  ○ Find: "[0-9][0-9].[0-9][0-9][0-9]"

  ○ Click: "Replace all"

- Repeat:

- Find: " --> \n >>"

- Replace: ">>"

- Click: "Replace all"

- NOTE: If this doesn't work, try replacing ">>" with "»" in both fields and adjusting the number of spaces before it in the "Find" field.

• Repeat:

- Find: "\n\n -->"

- Click: "Replace all"

- NOTE: Make sure the previous content in the "Replace" field is deleted. You may again need to play with the number of line breaks ("\n") or spaces in the "Find" field.

• Repeat:

- Find: " "

- Replace: " "

- Click: "Replace all"

- Click: "Replace all" again

• You should now have a relatively clean transcript. If it doesn't look perfect, that's okay!

You can now use this cleaned transcript instead of the auto-generated captions.

Step 3: Upload the recording to YouTube.

• Log into your YouTube Channel. (If you do not have one, create a free account.)

- If necessary, trim the video. You may choose to cut out the pre-event chit chat.

- Upload the video to the YouTube channel.

- Write a video description. In this space you can also include a link to the clean transcript Google Doc.

- Download the clean Google Doc transcript as .txt file (File > Download > Plain text)

- Go to the subtitles section on YouTube and upload the .txt file. (Choose the option to sync automatically without timestamps.)

- Once you are happy with how everything is set up, mark the video as public.

- You can now share the video link and also grab the embed code from YouTube and embed the video on your website.

SCHEDULING

You will never schedule your event at a time that will be ideal for everyone. People have a variety of work schedules, caregiving responsibilities, travel plans, religious holidays, and preferences. The timing of the event greatly influences how inclusive your event will be. Your target audience will be key in making this decision. If it is midday, people might not be able to leave their 9-to-5 office job to attend. If it is after 9-to-5 work hours, parents or people who have caregiving responsibilities might not be able to attend. Facilities might not be free or available on weekends. Friday nights can prevent observant Jewish attendees from coming and Sunday mornings could prevent various Christian attendees. There will never be a perfect time for the event, so think about the group you are hoping to target. Some factors to consider:

- Do the dates conflict with another conference or major event for my field or for the target group of event participants?

- Would the event happen during an important festival or holiday in the location of the conference and thus drive up the cost of hotel rooms and travel tickets?

- If there are public transportation options to the venue, is the event occurring during operational hours or will the subway be closed and buses no longer available?

- Do certain dates drive up venue costs?

ORGANIZING ALONE OR WITH A TEAM

You might decide to organize events by yourself or as part of a team. Both strategies have benefits. When organizing alone, you have a lot more control over the design and execution of the event. On the other hand, having a partner or organizational team means that you can divide tasks and work amongst members. However, being able to trust your co-organizers and knowing you can depend on people to complete their tasks is key for a smooth collaboration. Since life happens and people might experience personal difficulties, have a plan for redistributing tasks if someone is no longer able to complete them. I recommend having a plan in place before anything wrong has happened; otherwise miscommunication during a tumultuous time can lead to hurt feelings and damaged relationships.

Even when organizing an event alone, you will likely still need to work with other people as part of the event. You might elect to hire staff or work with volunteers to assist with recording the event or the marketing of the event. You might also decide to work with community partners such as community organizations or local businesses.

Community Partners

Have you considered working with a community partner? Co-hosting events or collaborating with others can amplify resources for your event. By working with organizations with similar values, you can expand your networks by sharing resources such as funding, equipment, and space. You and your community partner can also leverage each other's networks for publicity, potentially increasing and diversifying your participant pool.

A co-hosted event often implies that all of the organizers are sharing the workload and investment of resources, whereas a collaboration might mean a smaller contribution from one or multiple partners. When working with community partners, it is beneficial to discuss how work and resources will be divided between everyone involved. Perhaps you will provide funding for the honorarium, video webinar fees, and CART captioner for the event and your partner will provide the room, take the lead on the publicity, and share their computer equipment. If your event is part of a series, perhaps you will cover the costs and organizational details for one event and your partner will take the lead on the second event. Being clear about your needs and expectations can lead to a smoother working relationship.

You may also elect to partner with another organization to use your platform to amplify the work of others. If you have an established outdoor film screening series, you might invite a community partner to curate the films for one week and make the introductory remarks at the event. By including a partner in this manner, you can expose your audience to the work of this partner organization.

Partnerships can be effective if there are logical connections between the partnering organizations. If you are curating an exhibit on HIV and AIDS activism within a queer archive, you might partner with a community health organization that provides patient affirming care and sexual health education to co-host a vernissage or launch party. Maybe it makes sense to work with several community partners at the same time so you can all bring different perspectives and resources to the table. Just make sure to maintain ongoing dialogue and transparency between organizing partners.

MONEY/COSTS

*I*s it possible to organize an event for zero dollars? Kinda. It is likely that money will be involved in conference organizing even if it is in the form of donations and/ or sweat equity. Your decisions around who gets paid, what you pay for, and whether or not you charge for tickets influence the inclusivity of the event.

Funding

You might be asking, how am I supposed to pay for all of this? What if you have to rent a venue, rent AV equipment, and pay performers?

I usually begin planning by imagining I have no budget at all and see what is possible with zero dollars. Then I work from there.

Tickets

Tickets are one way to fund an event. Selling tickets or having conference registration fees, in advance of your event, can help you have a better sense of your budget and make sure that you aren't exceeding the capacity of your venue. Since some folks likely will not show up at the last minute or not attend every event at the conference you can sell a few tickets over your capacity limit (around 5-8% over), however you want to stick close to the venue capacity. There are numerous online platforms that can facilitate registration and ticketing, such as Eventbrite. However, many platforms take a cut of the sale. Read the fine print. Furthermore, not everyone has a credit card. Will you share an alternative way for people without credit cards to buy tickets in advance?

Selling tickets at the door is a low-tech way to handle sales, but not everyone carries cash, so you might need a PayPal linked to a QR code, a credit card processing app such as Square, or a similar app to accept door registrations. In your publicity for the event, explain what kinds of options will be available and whether or not tickets will be available at the door.

Tickets can also create barriers to access as not everyone can afford to attend every event. One solution is Pay What You Can (PWYC) or "Nobody Turned Away for Lack of Funds." Sliding scales can be useful or consider tiered ticket prices, such as "students and elders pay a lower ticket price." Another option can be to have scholarships available for some people to attend; this option can be especially useful for events such as conferences in which people may need to travel from out of town as the registration fee is usually not the only cost to participate.

You might be able to receive donations for your event. Donated space. Donated performances. Volunteer workers.

If your event is a fundraiser, people may be more amenable to donating time and resources. Fundraisers usually still have some form of ticket or collection of a resource (money, cans, and/or labor).

Sponsors and Grants

Sponsors can be another funding option. As an event organizer, you need to decide if you are comfortable taking sponsorships. Likely accepting sponsorships will entail that you advertise for the company, which might feel inappropriate depending on your event. Remember that you are in control of what kinds of companies and organizations you take money from. Maybe there is a local business that reflects your values and would sponsor your event? These partnerships can put your audience in connection with local businesses or channel corporate money towards a cause you believe in.

Local businesses and organizations may also be able to provide in-kind funding by donating space, staff, technological equipment, food, drinks, expertise, or other materials. For community organizations with values aligned with your own and who would also benefit from a collaboration, perhaps you can share resources and draw attention to the organization's work during your event.

If your conference is associated with an organization, that organization might already have funds that can be allocated towards the event or conference. Member dues often help subsidize events and conferences.

Universities and colleges can be a great source of funding for events. Even if you are not a student, is it possible to work with a local student group? They often are able to get student activities funding that can pay for speakers, artists, musicians, and performers.

Municipal funding is another great option. It is likely that your town or city has some form of funding available for local events programming. Does your event idea relate to any local community initiatives? Is there a festival, theme, or goal of your municipal government? State, provincial, territorial, and regional funding is a similar option. Many states and provinces offer grants. Consider potential limitations to receiving this type of funding, and how state and municipal control can limit the message or effectiveness of your conference.

National and international grants can be more complex, but depending on your project, can be another option. It is important to note that these kinds of grant applications can require hundreds of pages of paperwork and might not be worth completing for some conferences. Check out what grants you are eligible for a year in advance of your conference.

While it is outside of the scope of this book to explain grant applications in full, Beth Pickens and Betty S. Lai have created useful materials for grant writing. You want to make sure that you communicate clearly what you need the money for to an audience that may not know your specific area of interest. Furthermore, make sure that your budget is clear and specific. It is useful to show other funding sources.

Foundation and private grants can vary in the kinds of application materials that they require. Money may be available for the kind of work that you are trying to do. Again, I would suggest applying to these kinds of grants after you are already comfortable organizing conferences as the applications ask about past experience.

Most grants require some form of matching funding. Check if the grant accepts in-kind matching funding. For example, if you plan to hold your event in donated space, with donated sound and camera equipment—all of that counts as in-kind funding.

A bit of money grows. Funding agencies are more likely to give money and support if they see that you have already gotten some form of funding and support. For example, my speaker and workshop series, Disrupting Disruptions, has received four Canadian Social Science and Humanities Research Council Connection Grants (each valued around $25,000 CAD). These grants require 50% matching funding, so $12,500 external funding.

If you are required to show matching funding, check if in-kind contributions can count. Funding partners are more likely to contribute funds and resources if you show that you already have support. Start by getting small contributions of $100 from local organizations. Then leverage this funding into contributions of $200 and then $500 and then larger contributions.

This process is time-intensive and may entail writing smaller grants to count towards the matching funding. The first time I used this tactic, I dedicated three months of my life to this unpaid work on top of my primary employment. Again, start small and you can build on this experience. It might seem counterintuitive, but the more grants you win, the more grants you are likely to win in the future. You will have proven that you are able to manage grant funding.

Event Organizers: Paid or Not Paid?

Being an event and conference organizer requires particular skillsets, can be time-consuming, and may be resource intensive. For example, organizing Disrupting Disruptions has meant that I collaborate with numerous community partners, train series crew members, run multiple social media accounts, build and maintain a website, apply for grants, handle accounting for several grants simultaneously, coordinate a publicity campaign, handle the tech for hybrid events, and then make materials available to the public after the event. With the crew members, I have to oversee paying them for their time training and for their labor assisting with the series, including their time sending emails related to the series. For every event, I reach out to the speaker, schedule the event, work with a staff member at my university to process paperwork to pay the honorarium, create a Facebook event page, create an Eventbrite page, set up a Zoom webinar, hire a CART human captioner through Canadian Hearing Services, fill out the paperwork to pay the CART captioner, and begin a publicity campaign on several social media platforms. Either I or one of my paid crew members does graphic design work to promote the events. We record the events and make the recording with the human-produced transcripts available on the series YouTube channel, which I maintain. I, then, embed the videos on the series website and publicize the recording.

As the series relies primarily on a type of grant which requires at least 50% matching funding, and I often work with under-resourced and underfinanced academic programs, arts organizations, and community organizations, I often have more than 10 community partners per SSHRC Connection Grant. Several of these partnerships require their own grant applications.

Each 90-minute event requires around 10 hours of work, meaning that for the first 96 events I hosted between January 2019 and April 2024, of the series I have dedicated around 960 hours organizing this series. Similarly for the average 2-day conference, I have typically spent around 200 hours organizing the event.

I have never been paid for organizing a conference and have volunteered this time. In part, this decision is due to the grants that I work with and my position within my university. However, even before my current position, I have volunteered this labor as the events might not have been able to occur if I did not donate the time. There are definitely times when I should have been paid for organizing events.

There are some circumstances in which organizers are paid for their labor. Organizing events and conferences is time-consuming.

Relying on volunteer labor limits who is able to do conference organizing work, and it can be a class issue. It is possible to set aside an honorarium, salary, or wages for organizers by building this expense into the budget and ticket prices, but be aware that some funding sources may prevent this option.

As a conference organizer, since I do not pay myself for my labor, I do not charge myself registration fees. If organizers are paid, that also might impact the decisions over whether or not the rest of the organizing crew is paid.

SPEAKERS/PERFORMERS

Choosing Who To Invite

If your event includes speakers, performers, or presenters of any kind, your choices over who to invite impacts the inclusivity of the event. Can you invite people from diverse backgrounds? Perhaps you have heard of the Tumblr account @AllMalePanels (AllMalePanels. Tumblr.com). The account highlights how often events about a large range of topics will only include men—and often only heterosexual, cisgender white men. Diversity is important because speakers and performers will draw on their expertise and lived experiences. Race, class, gender, sexual orientation, disability, ethnicity, and age are important factors to consider, but they are not the only ones. For example, if you are hosting an event with multiple speakers, can you include people at different stages in their career?

Valuing diversity is not the same as tokenization. Tokenization is the process of hiring and using an individual as a symbol of inclusion or compliance with regulations to avoid the appearance of discrimination or prejudice, without actually valuing that person's individual contributions and seeing their work as meaningful. To include a diverse array of speakers, performers, or presents, you might need to connect with other networks to invite folks outside of your own community, but these efforts are well worth it! Including a diversity of perspectives and backgrounds will enrich conversations and programming, as well as draw attention and interest from more diverse audiences.

Payment of Speakers and Performers

If your event involves artists, musicians, performers, speakers, or presenters, it is important to recognize that not paying for art and work is a class issue. Only people with financial flexibility and class privilege will be able to routinely work without pay, and this limits the kind of art, performance, and ideas that are displayed. As class in the United States and Canada is racialized and gendered, the voices, perspectives, and art of people of color, Indigenous people, women, non-binary people, and trans individuals are less likely to be showcased.

This is not to say that people will not volunteer their time and efforts to showcase their work, but if you are paying the venue and vendors, as well as making money as the organizer, it is important that the artists, performers, and/or speakers are paid. Exposure does not pay the rent.

Whenever I contact potential lecturers, panelists, or performers, in the initial email, I always mention compensation. As an organizer, you may have a limited budget. It is important to be honest and forthcoming about what you can pay the people that you are contacting. This way they can decide if the amount is acceptable to them. It is also important to think critically about the amounts you are offering various performers. Women, Indigenous people, and folks of color continue to be paid at lower rates for their work. Be transparent with how you are paying folks. Will you provide a lump-sum honorarium and if travel is necessary, have the presenters arrange their own accommodations? Will you cover travel, including a per diem, a daily allowance to cover food?

In addition, there is a difference between financial compensation and honorarium gifts. It is common practice to provide honorarium gifts to Indigenous elders or knowledge keepers as a sign of reciprocity and respect. These gifts, which may include tobacco, blankets, or other items, should be culturally appropriate. Check local resources to learn more about the proper protocols in your region.

Paying people promptly is important. Oftentimes, people are asked to front the money for their own work and have to wait months to be reimbursed. If you can book the travel for them or have a check or form of payment for performers the day of the event, that is best practice (though depending on your funding, not always possible). If you are working with university funding, payment can be notoriously slow; again, try to be transparent with the folks you are working with about payment timelines.

The speaker/artist/presenter may also choose to negotiate the pay. It is okay if you are not able to pay them more to say, "No, thank you." I find being upfront and honest about the budget leads to productive and cooperative discussions.

On occasion, performers/speakers may prefer to donate money on their behalf to a cause of their choosing. You can make this option available to them.

Template for Initial Contact Email (with details for performers from out of town)

*D*ear _____ (name),

My name is _____ (mention organizational affiliation here, if it pertains). I am the organizer of the

_____ *(event)*, which is _____ *(one to two sentences of background information about the event)*, taking place on _____ *(time and date—if this is flexible, mention potential dates but state that they are flexible)* at _____ *(place)*. I was wondering if you were interested in _____ *(the type of performance, talk, exhibit, etc.)*. We would be able to offer you _____ *(amount of money)* and cover your travel, including hotel stay and a per diem _____. *(Consider if a speaker or performer is coming from out of town how you will pay for their plane/train/gas, lodging, transportation, and a potential per diem)*.

(You can add a sentence here about the date that you would like for them to reply to you by.)

Thank you for your time and consideration,

_____ *(your name)*

I like to keep this initial email quite short. In further emails, it is useful to ask the speaker about the kinds of AV equipment that may be required and if they are comfortable with you filming, photographing, recording, live streaming, or broadcasting the event. You may request slides or a speech prior to the event in order to provide large-print access copies, although I do not tend to include this question in the initial email. If you don't know them, you can also ask the speaker's pronouns. However, if you need the event to be recorded to fulfill an organizational or grant mandate, mention this fact in the first email so the person can make an informed decision.

Conference Speakers and Payment

As an organizer you will need to make decisions over what kinds of labor you pay for during your events. Different kinds of events have different types of traditional protocols, which you might decide to challenge so that your event reflects your values. For example, for conferences it is typical practice that people who have applied to present during workshops, roundtables, and panels are not paid. In fact, usually presenters still pay conference registration fees, as it is common that most participants are also presenters. However, if you invite someone specifically to travel to speak at your conference, it is typical to offer that person an honorarium, such as a keynote speaker. Performers may or may not be paid depending on the context of their performance.

LANGUAGE/ COMMUNICATION

*L*anguage has the potential to expand or limit the accessibility of an event or conference. What is the primary language of your event? If you live in a multilingual area, will you offer interpretation? Will you have presenters, performers, or attendees that can only participate if there are sign language interpreters or CART captioning? How have you described your event on your signs, flyers, website, listserv emails, and/or social media posts? When you make introductory remarks to the audience will you use gender-inclusive language such as "Welcome everyone! Thank you for joining us tonight!" (Using a phrase such as "Welcome, ladies and gentlemen" excludes non-binary and gender non-conforming participants.) Even the name of your event can influence people's decisions over whether or not to participate, so it is important to think about your title, marketing, and use of language as a whole.

Introductory Remarks and Checking Pronunciation

Before the event begins, encourage anyone making introductions for presenters to check how people pronounce their names and their pronouns before introducing them to the stage. Even if someone's name pronunciation seems obvious to you, I still recommend double-checking pronunciation. If you are hosting the event in an unfamiliar location, practice the pronunciation of the nations and peoples mentioned in your land acknowledgement. Make sure you have the right acronyms and organization names, especially of your sponsors or co-collaborators.

Gender-Inclusive Language

Using gender-inclusive language, sometimes referred to as gender-neutral language, means that the language does not perpetuate gender stereotypes. Examples include neutralizing any reference to gender or sex and avoiding terms and phrases that reinforce a binary understanding of gender. Rather than saying, "Hello, ladies and fellas" you might say "Hello, folks." You can refer to folks with genderless titles such as *bartender* over *barman* or *flight attendant* over *stewardess*. You can incorporate gender-inclusive language throughout all stages of your event organizing. You can use it in emails with potential presenters, sponsors, and event partners. How can you make your language more gender-inclusive in your advertising materials, listserv emails, your website, and other forms of outreach? During your opening remarks, while facilitating the Q&A period you can use gender-inclusive language while interacting with all presenters and participants. Furthermore, as a general rule, do not assume anyone's gender and pronouns.

Plain Language

Using plain language is another technique to make your event language more accessible. It is a form of writing that makes important information and ideas more accessible to people with intellectual and developmental disabilities, and others with disabilities affecting reading, comprehension, and other cognitive functions. As disabled journalist Andrew Pulrang explains, plain-language writing includes various approaches, such as . . .

- using common words and words with fewer syllables;
- using shorter sentences and paragraphs;
- using active instead of passive voice;
- and cutting back on extra details or personal impressions.

Plain-language writing can also be useful for people who are participating at the event or with event materials in a second language.

Consider utilizing plain-language in publicity and advertising materials. If you are going to have two versions of your materials, the complete information of the original document should be included in the plain-language version, yet it should be written in a more accessible way. As Zoe Gross of the Autistic Self Advocacy Network says, "A plain-language translation of a complex document should be a true translation: it should contain the same complex ideas and content expressed in a more accessible way, rather than removing ideas until things seem more simple." Being intentional with your words can expand accessibility.

Interpreters and Captioning

Interpreters work with spoken or signed words, conveying a message from one language to another (including sign languages). Translation deals with written texts. Your event may require both interpreters and translators.

I live in Montréal, Canada. Québec is a francophone province and many of our events are bilingual (French and English). I grew up in Southern California where many events included English and Spanish programming. It's also important to note that even when the event has materials and presentations in the most commonly spoken languages, speakers from other language groups can be left out.

Deaf and hard of hearing participants may require an interpreter. The location of your event and your target audience will determine your interpretation and translation needs. Make sure that sign language interpreters on a stage are well lit so that audience members are able to see them.

There are international, national, and more local resources for finding interpreters and translators. Internationally, the International Association of Conference Interpreters provides a great tool to find certified professionals (AIIC.net). In Canada, the Canadian Translators, Terminologists and Interpreters Council provides a database for certified professionals outside of Québec (CTTC.org/chercher.asp). Within Québec, see OTTIAQ.org. If you are looking for a translator in the United States, you can also use the American Translators Association (ATANET.org).

Human CART captioners can provide live captioning. Canadian Hearing Services (CHS.ca) is a reliable CART service. While auto-captioning tools do not replace real-time interpretation, these tools can assist in making events more accessible. PowerPoint and Google Slides offer auto-transcription tools. Microsoft offers an automated translation plug-in which functions as an auto-captioning device when "interpreting" from the presenter's language to the same language, such as English to English. This tool also provides a short url where participants can select their preferred language to follow along on their own devices.

If you aim to reach potential event participants who come from different language communities, create either multilingual publicity materials or different versions of your publicity materials in different languages. On your posters, social media posts, and registration pages you might include the information about the event in two or more languages. You can work with a human translator. While DeepL and Google Translate have improved over the years, if you do not speak the language you are writing in, check with someone who does to make sure that your materials are conveying the message that you desire.

Q&A Periods

After lectures, panels, roundtables, and workshops, audience question and answer (Q&A) periods are common practice. During these Q&A periods, there is a tendency for people with more privilege to raise their hands first and dominate the microphone. It can be useful to remind people to be aware of the space that they are occupying in the room. If as an organizer you are the one choosing who is asking questions, think about the demographics of the people who are asking most of the questions.

By providing a short pause of two minutes between the performance/talk and the Q&A period, people will have time to gather their thoughts and reflect upon their questions before asking them. If there is a panel chair, the chair will likely start the question period with one of their own in order to ease the audience into the Q&A period.

If you have a microphone, either have audience members line up to ask their questions into the microphone or pass the microphone to them so that people who are hard of hearing can hear. If there is no microphone for audience questions, please ask that the person answering the question repeat the question before answering it.

If you are worried about encountering the dreaded "more of a comment than a question," no questions from shy audience members, or the possibility of trolling and/or harassment at the event, it is possible to collect audience questions in advance or pass a hat to collect questions. This method also serves as a way you can filter some of the questions if there is a risk of hostile participants. If your event is happening in a digital space, it is possible to filter questions similarly by asking people to send their questions in advance or through an online platform.

For in-person events, Kim TallBear, a Sisseton-Wahpeton Oyate professor of Indigenous Studies, has recommended encouraging audience members to workshop their question idea with the people sitting next to them during a two-minute pause before the Q&A period begins. She finds that by encouraging participants to connect with folks nearby, audience members are less likely to ask hostile, racist, or meandering questions. This practice can also encourage socializing among participants.

A Q&A period can also be wonderful for audience members to connect with the speaker. However, it is important to set a timeframe. Many of us have encountered a Q&A period that seems to go on and on and on. Too-long Q&A sessions can be hard on an audience and a speaker. Check in advance with your speaker if perhaps questions can continue in a more informal way after the event.

PUBLICITY/ADVERTISING

*W*hen you organize events you will have spent significant time making arrangements; it is important that people are able to benefit from all of your labor. In order for people to come, they will need to know that the event is happening. Publicity for your event enables you to share important practical details such as location, date, and time, while also communicating the ethos of your event.

How will you publicize your event? In the pages to come, we'll discuss a wide variety of techniques that use different forms of technology. The following section is organized from analogue to digital publicity techniques.

Word of Mouth

Word of mouth is a low-tech way of sharing information about an event. This strategy can be effective if you have an already established network of participants. This strategy mostly involves talking to people. If you are looking to reach broader audiences, you will need to use additional strategies. Word of mouth is most effective when paired with other techniques.

Invitations: By Snail Mail or Email

Will you send a personal invitation to every person you'd like to attend? Will you send a card or letter? Handwritten invitations sent via the post office in particular are likely to stand out in the era of digital media, but you will have to budget for postage and stationery. Furthermore, you will have to take into account delivery times. If you need to send the card before every event detail is finalized, you can direct attendees to a website or social media page.

Emails are a cheaper method of publicity, yet still can be time-consuming. While a single email sent on a listserv will only require writing up a few sentences and perhaps linking to a poster file or info packet, personalized emails can be far more time-intensive. While mass emails may go to SPAM boxes and listserv emails may be ignored, a personalized email could be an effective strategy if there is someone in particular that you really want to attend.

Whether you use snail mail or email and personalized or mass messages, it is useful to collect information about people's intent to attend. You can include RSVP cards with snail mail or include a QR code or link that has people confirm their attendance. With emails, you can link to a calendar invite or a registration form.

Posters and Flyering

Posters and flyering is a publicity technique that involves creating printed materials that you distribute or post in different physical locations. Flyering and postering involve a number of steps:

- writing copy (the text for the poster),
- graphic design and layout,
- and taking the time to physically go to the locations where you will . . .
- tape, staple, pin, or nail the flyer.

Posting on public cork bulletin boards and taping flyers to streetlights can be an effective method of information-sharing if you are trying to attract event participants within a smaller geographic area where the flyers can reach. However, be mindful of municipal regulations as unapproved flyering can result in fines. Some communities have designated spaces for flyers and posters.

The benefit of this advertising technique is that people might stumble upon your event by chance. For people without social media, email addresses, mobile electronic devices, computers, or stable Internet access, posters and flyers can be a useful way to reach them. Even if passersby do not ultimately participate in this specific event, your poster or flyer can raise awareness about organizations they might not have previously known about. Furthermore, if your event centers on a marginalized community such as a Latinx dance performance, a reading by Black trans short story authors, a Queer Wine Drink and Paint night, or a panel about decolonizing foodways by Indigenous chefs, there is value in people from those communities seeing the poster even if they cannot attend that particular event. In short, posters and flyers act as a form of media representation.

Printing black-ink posters is one of the cheapest options. If you want a pop of color but do not have the funds to print with color ink, print your poster on brightly colored paper. Using a large, sans-serif font with a high level of contrast against the background is useful for people with dyslexia and people with reduced vision. Signage, presentations, and written materials should also have sufficient contrast levels. And of course, always use inclusive language.

When you design physical posters, you can also create a digital version for distribution on listservs and social media.

Social Media

Social media can be a low cost but potentially time-intensive strategy for publicity and communication. Most social media platforms do not require fees to participate, although you cede your data. The algorithms, or mathematical models, underlying data extraction and the repurposing of data by social media platforms have the ability to intensify social inequalities. While it is outside the scope of this book to discuss the social, environmental, and cultural impacts of Big Data, AI, and data extraction, see DisruptingDisruptions.com and click the video tab to watch recordings from activists, artists, and scholars discussing the ways in which these technologies disproportionately harm marginalized communities and contribute to environmental destruction through mining, water, and energy use. In addition to the environmental, social, and cultural impacts linked to social media's data extraction, you do not have full control over most of your social media accounts. These proprietary platforms can decide to sell to another company at a moment's notice, terminate your account for any reason, or decide to censor your posts.

Social media work can also be time-consuming. Establishing accounts, regularly posting, and gaming the ever-changing algorithms to make sure the folks see your event publicity—all of it takes energy. However, as many people use social media, it might be worth it as a strategy, especially when paired with other publicity techniques. Furthermore, social media platforms often have a feature for direct messaging. Depending on the privacy settings that you select on the platform, this feature allows people to write directly to you, which can facilitate contact with journalists for interviews.

For your event's social media strategy, you need to decide if you will use your own personal accounts or if it is worth establishing a special account or page for the event. If you already have personal social media accounts, are you comfortable sharing event information on them, as doing so might bring more attention to you? Will you change your personal account's privacy settings? Some social media platforms such as Facebook have Events, pages where you can create a listing for a single public event while maintaining your preferred privacy settings on your personal account. If your event will be part of a recurring series or if your event is a conference, I recommend establishing social media accounts for the series or conference in addition to the conference website. Here you can share graphics and photos before, during, and after the series' events or conference. Creating this online presence is especially useful if you plan to have additional iterations of your conference or to release publications based on the conference proceedings.

You do not need to use every social media platform. Choose platform(s) where your community and targeted participant group are already gathering. To gain more followers to spread awareness of your event, collaborate with other accounts to cross post information. Make use of your already established connections! But also think beyond them—can you cross promote your event with different organizations, social media pages, or listservs to increase the reach of your event and to diversify your participant pool?

Website

Depending on the size of your event and whether or not it is recurring, it may be useful to design a website. See the conference section for more information about designing a website.

Working with Journalists

Depending on your event, you might be able to garner publicity before or after it happens by working with journalists. You can try reaching out to journalists who cover similar events and subject matter via email or on their social media. It will help to have an established social media account, website, and other materials that you can share with journalists. If you have a website, have a section dedicated to media with a press kit where you can upload a PDF of press materials. This press kit will include your contact information, information about the event, and information about the organizers. The first page should show your press release, which is a one-page summary of everything else in the kit. Include photos and images that represent your event, with image permission information listed.

If you would like to have the event covered by the press, offer free press passes to journalists to attend the event. Even if journalists are interested in the event and even if they attend, you are not guaranteed to have press coverage as editorial decisions, breaking news, and a variety of other factors impact what is published or makes it to the air. It is useful to begin reaching out to journalists weeks in advance of the event.

Paid Advertising

Several social media platforms have the option for you to pay to "boost" a post so that it is seen by wider networks. Depending on the goals you have with your event, you might consider a paid post. You can also pay for advertising in periodicals, newspapers, podcasts, radio spots, YouTube advertisements, and internet banner ads—as well as the most expensive option, broadcast television. Some folks also pay social media influencers to do a sponsored post as this form of marketing apparently is more effective than traditional marketing techniques. However, it is likely that by relying on the free or low cost options already discussed above, you will reach your desired audiences.

Event Aesthetics and Design

While not required, I recommend deciding early on in your planning process what your event aesthetics are. For a single, one-off event, aesthetics are a bit less important than if you are planning a recurring series of events or a larger conference or convention. It can be useful to have visual coherence between the posters, social media posts, website, forms, and/or marketing. Even picking a color scheme and a font can bring a lot of unity to your publicity and communications. I recommend being intentional with your choices as colors and font convey specific vibes to potential conference participants.

Having a design aesthetic can distinguish your posts on social media and help participants identify your materials. Furthermore, having already made these design choices early on can save time later when you are doing design work for the conference.

You can create a logo or a tagline and use this on conference publications, SWAG, merchandise, and volunteer t-shirts. Creating a cohesive design template can make the conference appear more organized.

Design aesthetics can also expand accessibility. On publicity materials and slides, using a large, sans-serif font with a high level of color contrast against the background is useful for people with dyslexia and people with reduced vision. Don't rely only on color to convey information so that your materials are accessible to people who are color-blind. For more information about accessible design aesthetics, the UK Home Office has created an infographic guide with tips for accessible graphic design and the Association of Registered Graphic Designers has a free, in-depth guide, *AccessAbility 2: A Practical Handbook on Accessible Graphic Design.*

CHILDCARE

*W*hile some events have the option for children to be involved in programming, it might be necessary to provide childcare as an option in order to make childfree events accessible to parents and other caregivers. Executive Director of The Visual Arts Centre in Montréal and art historian Amber Berson, curator and arts administrator Juliana Driever, and their collaborators have created resources and artistic works, under the name "The Let Down Reflex," discussing the exclusion of parents from arts spaces, events, and conferences. They emphasize that being engaged with your community (including being at events and conferences) and being an engaged parent need not be mutually exclusive things. Let's not perpetuate the exclusion of parents and caregivers from conference spaces.

If the event can include children, indicate this information on your communications materials such as posters, social media posts, listserv emails, your registration page, and/or your event website. It is useful to include information about the the following:

- kinds of child-friendly activities your event will have,

- noise levels, and

- spaces for stroller parking, chestfeeding/breastfeeding, diaper stations in bathrooms, and play areas.

Also, consider:

- If you will be serving food and drinks, will you have food and drinks that may appeal to children?

- For longer events or conferences, will you have a refrigerator for breast milk and a space to prepare formula?

If not every aspect of your event is appropriate for children, you may want to provide childcare on site. Furthermore, if your event is not child-friendly, make that clear in your promotional materials.

You can ask people to RSVP in advance if they require childcare to be able to participate. There are several options for providing childcare. See if your town or city has an organization that subsidizes childcare. See if your venue has childcare options or has already partnered with a childcare provider. You will need to decide whether you plan to hire an outside firm of professional sitters or childcare providers or run the program yourself. It is important to be transparent about costs. Will participants have to pay to use the childcare services or will childcare be provided at no additional cost as part of the event? What age will childcare be provided for; the younger the child, the more supervision is required. If you are unable to provide childcare for the event or conference, offering to connect parents who would like to bring their children to the event or conference can also make pooling resources more possible.

DESIGNATED AREAS

*D*epending on the length and type of your event, you may require different designated areas. Below are key spaces to consider, whether they are separate rooms, areas within a room, or spots in a field during an outdoor event.

Washrooms/Bathrooms

If the venue already has all-gender and/or single-use washrooms, include this information on your conference website and map of the site. If the venue does not already have these kinds of washrooms, see if you can add signage to create an all-gender washroom for the duration of your conference.

Are there free tampons and pads available in the washrooms already? If not, put a basket in the washrooms with free menstrual products during the conference.

Will the venue make sure that toilet paper is restocked? If not, make sure to have additional toilet paper to restock bathrooms.

It is also helpful to let attendees know where potable water is available.

Chestfeeding/Breastfeeding Space

Is there a space for people to pump and store milk? If so, make this information available on your website. If the venue does not already provide this space, find a space within your venue. Is there a space to prepare formula for children on site?

Chill-Out Space

Is there a space where participants can chill out? Long events such as all-day workshops and conferences can be intellectually stimulating and exciting! They can also be really tiring, emotional, and exhausting. Is there a space at your venue with comfy chairs, quiet spaces, and natural lighting where people can decompress from sensory overload? If not at your venue, can you indicate a chill space in your program where participants may want to visit? While participants are capable of doing their own research, it is often appreciated to know that someone has already found some nearby locations.

Networking and Socializing Space

While panels, workshops, keynotes, and performances are exhilarating, longer events such as conferences are about more than the programmed events. Magic can happen over chance meetings, conversations after a particularly stimulating Q&A period, and even scheduled coffee meet ups. Do you have spaces at your venue where people are encouraged to gather with tables, chairs, and nearby refreshments?

Staging Area/Crew and Volunteer Area

Depending on the venue of your event, you likely will have a room or space where you store materials that need to be used during it. If you are hosting a short film screening, followed by Q &A or a lecture, you might be able to stash gear, bags, and other materials in a corner. However, for longer events or conferences it is useful to have a designated space for organizers to leave materials. For example, you might not want every program or SWAG right at the check-in desk. You might need to store some technological equipment. It also might be a space where your conference crew or volunteers can store their stuff, check the shift schedule, rest, and/or get snacks, drinks, or meals. Having an extra store of pens, pencils, paper, and tape can be useful. A first aid kit, extra toilet paper and sanitary products, and other materials you might need to restock (in case the venue does not already do this for you) are useful to store here too.

Bookseller and/or Vendor Area

If your event has booksellers or other vendors, it is important to find a location for them where they can get foot traffic, that will also not cause traffic jams in the conference space. Is there a space at your venue that promotes circulation, where participants can flow in and out (maybe with separate entrance and exit doors)?

Try not to put the vendors in the basement (unless the whole conference is also in the basement)! While every venue has its restrictions, hiding the vendors in the basement with no windows, no natural light, and a lack of natural foot traffic can be demoralizing for them. You want to make sure that everyone can have a good event experience.

In advance of the event, contact your vendors about their needs. Do they need electricity? Will they be bringing their own tables?

If your event has booksellers and some of the authors are event participants, is there a way to set up book signings or author talks in the same space where the vendors are so that the books are close at hand? Could you set up some chairs and a microphone in the vendor area or close to it for those kinds of events? Connect the bookseller with these authors so they can try to stock books in advance.

If you have a multi-day conference, showcase, or convention, is there a way the vendors can store their materials overnight? Packing in and out each day can be time-consuming and physically challenging for some vendors. If you have a single vendor or two in a room with a lock, can they store their materials in the locked room overnight?

FOOD/DRINKS

*D*oes your event involve food? Choices over food and drink can impact the accessibility of your event. Will you be working with caterers? Cooking together?

Food

Will you provide food at your event? Food can be a lovely way to build community. For day-long or multiday events, I like providing breakfast to participants as part of their registration. I find having a communal breakfast encourages people to arrive for morning events and can serve as an ice breaker.

If you are working with caterers, is there a way to incorporate their labor into the conference itself? If your conference is about food or small business, can you offer the caterers an honorarium to speak from their own experience? While this strategy might not be appropriate for every conference, I also appreciate how these kinds of morning events showcase different ways of knowing about a topic and can bring different members of a community together.

Will you be charging for the food? Cost of food can impact accessibility for participation and is a class issue. However, cheap food usually means that the farm workers, the people working in the food processing plants, the people cooking the food, and/or the people selling the food are not paid a living wage. This is a labor issue. This is also a feminist issue as women disproportionately do the underpaid or unpaid work of preparing food. Furthermore this labor is highly racialized and classed and is intertwined with immigration policies that criminalize workers. Cheap food comes at environmental costs under industrialized food systems that disregard biodiversity, use pesticides, and lead to the destruction of ecosystems. It is a difficult balance to make sure that food is priced so that every worker is properly compensated and that all participants can afford the food. There is rampant cruelty, exploitation, and injustice throughout the food chain, even when serving vegan food. Mixing the price of items available can be one way to address these issues. For example, you might include an inexpensive or pay-what-you-can soup alongside other higher-cost items.

Perhaps you will invite local food trucks or vendors to come to the event. Food can be a great way to involve local small businesses to participate. Be deliberate about the kinds of caterers and food vendors you invite. How do these businesses reflect the ethos of your event?

If you will have a snack table with free treats throughout the day, try to make sure that there is a variety of foods.

When serving food, there are dietary considerations such as vegan, vegetarian, kosher, and halal, as well as common allergens such as nuts, gluten, and soy. If the event involves a caterer, I try to order food that will meet as many dietary considerations as possible at once. Tasty vegan food with a gluten free option tends to accommodate most participants. However, food carries cultural significance. Depending on your event's objectives, you may make different choices surrounding food. Make sure to label food; you will save yourself from having to answer repeated questions about the food and people will be able to make informed decisions about what they are eating.

When participants register for the event, you can add a question on the registration form to ask about any dietary needs.

Drinks and Alcohol

Will you be serving alcohol at your event? The choice to serve alcohol may limit the age of participants for the event. It can also impact who might feel welcome to attend the event. People who wish to stay sober may refrain from attending. I recommend having a variety of events so that people who choose not to drink are also able to participate in some social activities related to the event. It is important to provide sober spaces.

The choice to serve alcohol may also require a permit. Check far in advance, as liquor permits can be difficult to obtain depending on your venue and city. Many regions also require certification for staff or volunteers to serve alcohol.

Have water available for free and encourage people to bring their reusable water bottles/containers. Restricting access to water can jeopardize the health of people attending the event. Depending on the venue, this may be more difficult due to the infrastructure of the facility. If there are no water fountains or if there is not running water available at the site, you may need to bring in water jugs for distribution.

Tips for Serving

These tips will encourage a more sustainable event.

- Single-use plastic plates and utensils go straight to the landfill. Is it possible to have food options that do not require utensils? Can you avoid using single-use items? Can you serve food on compostable plates?

- Encourage participants to bring reusable cups and water bottles.

- Have some straws available for participants who may require them to eat or drink.

- Ensure that food is clearly labeled (vegan, gluten-free, kosher, halal, etc) and mark common allergens.

- Have a recycling and compost bin in addition to a trashcan to reduce the environmental impact from the event. Make sure these are well marked. Assign a member of your conference crew to make sure these receptacles are emptied so people have space to properly dispose of their materials.

TECH/IT

*W*hen used with deliberate intention, technology has the potential of expanding the accessibility of our events. Tech is always transforming so while specific platforms mentioned below may change, the general advice remains.

Gear and AV Equipment
It is likely that your conference will require some kind of electronic equipment. If people are speaking, microphones can improve sound quality and projections. People giving a presentation might want a screen to project a slideshow. Maybe you will show a film or several shorts. Perhaps a band or DJ will play. You may choose to film, record, or livestream the event so that people who cannot attend can still access the event. Decisions surrounding AV equipment can either radically expand or decrease accessibility.

Using AV Equipment to Increase Accessibility
If there is a projection, such as a PowerPoint, Google Slides, or Prezi presentation, does the font contrast with the background? Is the font large and clear to read? Encourage presenters to orally describe what is on the slides. This technique is beneficial for participants that have reduced vision or are blind. It is also a useful practice if the event is being audio recorded.

Consider asking speakers to submit materials in advance of the event; this measure makes the event more inclusive for individuals who may not be able to view screens. Along this line, making printed copies available (in larger fonts) can be beneficial. You can also encourage presenters to include a QR code or tiny URL link directing participants to a copy of the slides so that they can read more closely or mark up and write notes with their own devices.

If your event or conference has panels, roundtables, or workshops with multiple presenters, it's best to require or strongly encourage folks in a session to put all of their slides into the same presentation (Google Slides can be a useful strategy for doing this). If not all in the same presentation, have everyone load their slides onto the same computer. Changing between computers (especially changing between Mac, Linux, and PC computers) can cause projection systems to fritz. By having all the slides in one spot, you can reduce friction and reduce stress from malfunctioning tech.

When playing videos, turn on closed auto-captioning. Or better yet, hire a CART captioner (although often priced at $335 for 2 hours of work, this option may not be financially possible). It is useful to check in with participants about their access needs in advance.

Ask presenters to use microphones and have the audience ask questions into a microphone or ask the presenter to repeat the question into the microphone. Speaking loudly is not the same.

Acoustics are important for those with hearing impairment. Limit unnecessary background noise.

Avoid using flashing or overly bright lights, as this can cause sensory overload.

Check if the facility has a hearing loop (sometimes called an audio induction loop). This is a special type of sound system for use by people who with hearing aids. The hearing loop provides a magnetic, wireless signal that is picked up by the hearing aid.

You can easily monitor sound levels/noise levels to make sure that your event will not lead to hearing damage. There are plenty of free sound level meter phone applications that you can download. Remember sound levels at or above 85 dB are dangerous and can cause hearing loss. Depending on your event, whether it is a lecture or a concert, you might play music at different levels; for example, if you want to encourage discussion, keep gentle background music at or below 60 dB.

If the wifi requires a password, print the wifi code prominently on the event or conference program if you have one. Have the wifi password or log on instructions posted around the venue. Make sure to have this information available at the check-in desk, if you have one. The easier it is for people to find the wifi information, the fewer questions you will have to answer about it.

How to Acquire or Rent AV Equipment

- First check out what the venue already provides for free. The venue may also offer rentals, which may or may not be the best deal but can potentially save time, hassle, and stress.

- If you are affiliated with a university, even if the event is not at a university, you usually have access to an AV room for free or inexpensive rentals. This equipment can range from microphones, video cameras, and more!

- Check out your local library for resources. Many have lending libraries with different kinds of equipment.

- Borrow from friends.

- If none of the above options work or if you need a particular piece of gear, private rental companies exist.

Ahead of the event, make sure that you have the batteries or power cords that you need for this equipment with you. If you are hosting your conference outside, you might need a generator.

Having an IT Crew on Site

While having a support crew to help with tech is useful, it can be equally important to have dedicated tech support on site, especially for a conference or a music festival. Does the venue already supply tech/IT support? For example, some music venues already have a sound and lighting team they will want you to work with. If your event is at a university, you might be able to work with the on site tech/IT department. If there is no on-site tech crew, make sure to work with your team in advance, practicing the tech.

Do a soundcheck and check all necessary technology before each event starts. If a video is embedded in a PowerPoint or similar presentation, have the room monitor work with the presenter to check that it works before their panel, roundtable, or workshop begins. There is still always a risk that the tech will fail. Have you made a backup plan? Encourage presenters to bring a printed copy of their notes.

Extra Tech Prep for Hybrid Events

Hybrid events are some of the most technically challenging event formats, especially for conferences. If you want to provide a good experience for in-person and virtual attendees, you will need to properly staff the physical and virtual rooms. I highly recommend having room monitors in each physical room for hybrid events.

Single Hybrid Stream

By a single hybrid stream event, I mean that you are only managing one event at a time; there are not multiple hybrid events happening concurrently. Are you hosting a fire-side chat in which the speakers are in a physical room together, but people can attend virtually? Are you hosting a panel where presenters and audience members are both in-person and virtual? Below I will provide instructions for setting up these kinds of events.

Option 1: All of the presenters are in the same room and attendees are both in-person and online

In advance of the day of the event:

- Create a registration page so you can distribute the webinar/video streaming link. It is useful to use a platform where you collect participants' email addresses so that you can keep the link private. If you decide to post the webinar/video streaming link publicly you, may increase your risk of zoombombing. Depending on the platform you use, you can enable security features so that you are essentially broadcasting a hybrid event but online participants will not be able to turn on their cameras, microphones, or use the chat. You may still elect to use a Q&A function on the platform even when the chat is closed.

- Create the Zoom webinar or set up the video link on the video chat platform you are using. You will need to enable the features that designate the presenters as panelists who can turn on their videos, microphones, and screen share.

- If you are using a human captioner or interpreter, book them. Once you have their contact information, set them up as captioners or interpreters within the webinar ahead of time. You might have to enable specific features on the platform. For example, Zoom webinars have a feature where a participant can be designated as an interpreter and during the event, participants can toggle between the different audio feeds. For sign language interpretation, you may need to have more than one interpreter for the event.

- Send the presenters their panelist links. Create a calendar invite (such as in Google Calendar) with each presenter's unique link included.

- Write and schedule emails with the webinar/video link to registered attendees through the registration system (if the platform that you are using has a feature that allows you to schedule emails). On the event registration page and in all my communications about the event, I also make the note that people will receive the webinar/video link three days before the event, again one day before the event, and finally 15 minutes before the event starts. Having these three emails serves to remind attendees and distribute the links to people who register closer to the event.

- If your event is part of a larger speaker series or affiliated with a conference or organization with the website, put the registration link on that website.

- As being the event organizer means I have to chat with several people before, during, and after an event and handle other matters simultaneously, I hire folks to work with me on the day of the event. I book one of my event organizing team members to assist with the event from 30 minutes before the event, during the event, and afterwards for the distribution of the recording (if you are recording the event). I pay them, at time of writing, $26.73 an hour plus 22.33% benefits (current minimum wage in Québec where I live is $16.10 an hour). I budget 3 to 3.5 hours of their labor for a 90 minute event and uploading of the video. If you do not have a budget, maybe a friend will volunteer to assist with the tech.

- I write out opening remarks, including the description of the speaker series, the procedure for the Q&A of the event, the speaker bio, and the land acknowledgement (this is especially important so the CART captioner can spell names correctly). If the event is co-hosted, the co-hosts and I divide the opening remarks in advance.

- A few days before the event I will reach out to the CART captioner and interpreter(s) with the link for my opening remarks document, their unique panelist links (on most platforms, captioners and interpreters will have unique links), and my phone number in case of tech issues. I also CC my team member on this email since they will need the captioner's email to later send the API token (access code) for captioning. This code will enable the captioner to type their captions into the webinar.

- A few days before the event, I also do a follow up with the speaker about their needs, share my cell number in case of tech issues, and follow up on emails from people asking questions about the event.

On the day of the event:

- Arrive 30 minutes before the event starts.

- If you are using a single computer for the event (recommended), connect it to the projector and sound system.

- Start the webinar/ virtual video session. With some platforms you can keep online participants in a waiting room while you are setting up the tech.

- If you are working with a CART captionist and/or interpreter(s), have them arrive 20-30 minutes before the event starts. You may need to enable captioning and interpretation settings within your video platform if you haven't already done so. The captionists and interpreters might need you to help them check their tech. You may have to send the captionist an API token (in this case, the caption URL) provided by the platform so that the captioner can caption the event.

- If you are relying on auto-captioning and the video platform doesn't already enable it, make sure to enable the captions. These captions will also show on the screen for in-person participants.

- Check that the screen share feature is functioning properly.

- Make sure presenters arrive at least 15 minutes early. After welcoming the presenter(s), have the presenter(s) check that their slides are functioning. If you are using the presenter's computer, hook their computer to the AV system so that they can screen share. This way, in-person attendees can see the slides projected and attendees in the virtual space can see the slides. Be aware that you might have to go into the presenter's computer's system preferences and change the screen mirroring configuration.

- Strongly encourage all presenters to use the same computer for their slides for a more frictionless event—changing between computers, especially from a Mac to PC to Linux can mess with projector and sound systems.

- If there is embedded sound or videos within the presenter's slideshows, make sure that the sound is working properly.

- Check that any links embedded in the slideshow are working. You may decide to pre-open the links for easier navigation during the event. If the presenter plans to navigate away from the slideshow at any point, it is advisable to select a screen share option that shows the presenter's entire screen rather than just the slideshow.

- Check that microphones are working properly and not creating reverb.

- If you have an OWL (a 360-degree camera, mic, and speaker device that was created to facilitate hybrid events), similar device, or other microphones in the room, make sure that the sound and video is working.

- Check in with the speaker to make sure you are properly pronouncing their name and the name of their institutions and projects for the introductions.

- Allow in-person participants to start to enter the room around 15 minutes before the event starts. If the weather outside is harsh, welcome participants early but warn them that they will see the tech setup (something folks often anticipate).

- As participants log into the webinar or video call, give them updates about when the event will start. Usually, I start hybrid events three minutes after the announced start time as people are looking for log in information and in-person attendees may arrive a few minutes late.

- I also enter the webinar or video call on my personal computer with the volume and microphone muted so that while in-person I can monitor the virtual experience and provide technical support. My team member also often has their computer logged in for the event.

- Before we start the event, I check in with the speaker, the captioner, interpreter, and whomever else I am working with that each person is ready to begin.

- We start the recording if the presenter has consented to a recording. We have chosen to record to the cloud because one time a team member's recording on their personal computer somehow got deleted. Note that a Zoom webinar account has a limited amount of storage but can easily hold a two-hour event recording.

- I or my co-host, if it is a co-hosted event, introduces the speaker, thanks sponsors, and shares information about accessibility.

- When I begin the opening remarks, the captioner will usually use the document I have provided with opening remarks to help with the beginning of the captioning.

- I also make sure that in-person attendees know they can ask questions by raising their hand at the end and virtual attendees can ask questions through the Q&A box. To prevent zoombombings, I turn off the ability for audience members to write in the chat, speak through mics, and turn on video. You should make decisions that make sense for your own community. You might need to set up this feature in advance depending on which platform you use. Either way, explain to participants the ways they can ask questions during or after the presentation.

- I try to move my gaze back and forth between the in-person audience and the computer's camera (and thus the online audience) so both groups of participants feel equally involved in the event.

- The presenter gives their talk or workshop. The presenter has full control over their computer and slides, but as an organizer I am there to assist. Forty-five minutes has been the sweet spot for the speaker series I run, but you know your community and what kind of event you want. Encourage the presenter to make eye contact with the in-person audience and the camera for the virtual attendees.

- During the event, I take screenshots of the webinar (and crop out the number of participants and their names). I also take photos of the event, but try to do so in a way that attendees are not identifiable in the pictures for privacy concerns.

- During the Q&A section, in-person and online participants are encouraged to ask questions. I ask that the presenter(s) repeat the in-person questions so that webinar/video call attendees can know what is being asked. My team member and I take turns asking the questions from the virtual Q&A box. We also often let people know in advance that we might combine some questions or might not be able to get to everyone's questions but we appreciate everyone's interest and participation.[1] We only read the first names of the zoom-question-askers aloud OR they are also able to ask questions anonymously. Some speakers also prefer to not have the Q&A part recorded.

- I wrap up the event by thanking the presenter, captioner, interpreters, team members, and attendees. I also sometimes plug upcoming events.

After the Event

- People might stick around in-person to mingle or ask the presenter more questions. Virtual participants tend to log off the moment the event concludes. Make sure to book the space for enough time so there can be 15 minutes of folks connecting and saying their goodbyes.

- I might have to clean the room or reorganize the chairs in the room after the event.

---

1 I started making this announcement after someone started to send me harassing messages because we did not get to their third question.

- After the event, we upload the video to our YouTube channel with the captions created by the professional human captioner. The human captioner's captions are much better quality than YouTube's auto-generated captions. I, then, embed the video recording into the speaker series website.

- I send the video recording link to everyone who registered and I also publicize the recording on social media.

- I share photos of the event to my speaker series' social media accounts.

- After the event, I follow up with the presenter and thank them. I also follow up to make sure that they have received their honorarium.

- Record the attendance data from the event to save for any reports you may have to submit to granting agencies or sponsors. It is useful to collect this information in case you plan to apply to future grants. You can also collect data on the number of video recording views.

I have described an event with one speaker. Panel events also can work in this format, but I recommend that all slides for every speaker are running off of one person's computer and ideally everyone can put their slides into a single slideshow (Google Slides makes this simple) in order to simplify tech requirements.

Option 2: Some of the presenters are in-person and some are online and attendees are both in-person and online

In this case, you will follow many of the same procedures as option 1; however, you will need to make sure to have the online presenters test their slides remotely before the event starts. Allow more time for the tech check as you cannot offer to change settings on their computer. Sometimes, there can be lag time between the presenter and the projection on the screen. If a presenter's wifi cuts out, have a backup plan in place. It is important to have presenters' phone numbers or other contact information.

Option 3: All of the presenters are online and attendees are in-person and online

Again, follow most of the steps from options 1 and 2 but you will need to make sure that you have enough time for each person to check their tech, and troubleshooting may take even longer. Use your own computer to connect to the projector system. You will need to sit at the front of the room near the screen to more readily facilitate questions.

Multi-Stream Hybrid Events

The following instructions are for hybrid multi-stream events such as conferences that have some rooms with in-person presenters and virtual attendees and some virtual presenters whose panel, workshop, or roundtable is being projected into a physical space at the conference.

You will not be able to be in every room as one individual. You will need to work with a team. The hybrid multi-stream event will work best if there are room monitors in each room. Make sure room monitors are in the room 15 minutes BEFORE the panel/workshop starts.

Room Monitoring with In-Person Presenters and Virtual Participants

These tips are also useful if you are having an in-person conference but recording all events by using a virtual meeting or webinar platform rather than having video cameras set up on a tripod in each room.

Have a computer connected to the Zoom meeting (or whichever platform you are using) in the room. In case Zoom feed disconnects, have a document named "Links" saved on the desktop of each computer with the Zoom links in it. The computer login and password should be written on the computer next to its keyboard.

The room monitors will need to assist the presenters getting their slides onto that computer (this way you don't have to have the presenters connected to Zoom on their own computers). Ask that presenters show up 15 minutes before their panel/workshop begins so they can get the tech set up with the room monitors.

As presenters have been instructed to email their slides, create a virtual link, or bring a USB stick (something I recommend doing), room monitors can help presenters move slides off of their computers. It is also useful to have a USB stick and a USB-C adaptor in each room that can assist presenters moving slides off their computers.

It is helpful if room monitors also bring their own computer, tablet, or phone to monitor either the chat or the Q&A box (if the chat has been closed for safety reasons). Monitors can ask questions to the in-person presenters from the virtual attendees. If room monitors do not have their own devices, as a conference organizer, consider making one available for them.

You can require that each panel, roundtable, workshop, or speaker is responsible for their own timekeeping. However, since the conference needs to make sure that the panel/Q&A session ends on time so that the next group of presenters can set up, the room monitor can facilitate this process.

Room Monitoring in Room with Virtual Panel Being Projected
  into the Conference

So that there is more of an interaction between virtual presenters and in-person participants, designate a room that will project the virtual presentations. The room monitor will be responsible for making sure that the livestream is projected into the room.

The room monitors should bring their own computer, tablet, or phone to monitor the chat so that they can ask questions from the in-person attendees and share them with the virtual presenters. It is useful to let the in-person attendees know that you will be doing this. People in the room can also be logged into the zoom webinar and type their own questions. Just make sure that their volume is off so that there is no reverb.

FACTORS YOU NEED TO CONSIDER FOR SPECIFIC EVENT TYPES

E vents can be everything and anything, but all have unique features. The below section has additional considerations for specific events.

Concerts and Battles of the Bands

Make sure to properly communicate with the band(s) about the length of their set lists. Allocate sufficient time for a soundcheck. If it is possible for some of the bands to share some gear, such as a drumset during a battle of bands, try to do so. If you are hosting a music festival or a show with many performers, is it possible to have more than one stage so that while one band is setting up its gear, another band can play. I highly recommend having at least one person (who is not the main event organizer) in charge of sound and lights.

Reading or Book Launch

If you are doing a reading to promote a book that will be for sale and the event is at a bookstore, make sure that the bookstore is able to put in the order for the books weeks in advance. If you are selling your own copies or working with a bookstore which will sell the books on consignment, make sure that you provide a sufficient number of copies. Check that you have microphones or a voice amplifier so that audience members can hear. Ideally you will also have a microphone to pass around the audience during the Q&A period. If not, make sure that the author repeats audience member questions before answering them so everyone can hear the responses.

Fair with Booths or Tables

Spacing of the booths and/or tables is important. You do not want there to be overcrowding but you also want to make sure that people are able to circulate without too long of distances between booths.

Lecture/Speaker

Speak with the presenter in advance about your expected schedule and how long to plan to present. Explain whether there will be tech support for a slideshow or sharing other materials. Preparing a 15-minute presentation is much different than a 45-minute one.

Parade or March

If your event is labeled as a parade or march, make sure to actually march. Having people gather under the hot sun or in the freezing cold to stand around when they are prepared to move (and dressed for that activity) is not a form of community care. It can be wonderful to plan to have a rally at a meeting point along the parade or march route so that people who are unable to move along the parade route due to different disabilities or scheduling can meet up with your group. Make sure that—if your parade or march is centered on a marginalized group—where you gather, you can make the meeting space safe or safer. For example, do not have people stand around unprotected in a space that is surrounded by hostile crowds OR if you know there will be a counter-protest, make sure to prepare participants for that reality. If people are giving speeches, have voice amplification and think about the role of language and interpretation, including sign language.

One example of a march that incorporates the principles of accessibility and social justice is the NYC Dyke March. The NYC Dyke March centers community care by having March Marshals. These marshals are trained volunteers, who can attend one of several training sessions and who are allocated roles such as . . .

- accessibility (assisting participants with disabilities)
- folks to walk in the back, right/left side, and front to provide protection and direct the crowd
- bike/runner (to communicate between the different marshals spread throughout the march)
- a troll patrol (to de-escalate confrontations with counter-protestors or people who harass the marchers)
- folks at the Washington Square Park gathering site, where the march culminates.

Dyke March NYC also has masked sections for their outdoor march in which all volunteers also mask. The organizers make clear what accessibility measures are already in place. They also share that requests can be made for free wheelchairs, sighted guides, cab funds for disabled people to get to and from the march, and

ASL interpretation at the march. Accessibility marshals are also available to push wheelchairs if needed and wanted and additional wheelchairs may be available on the day of the march for last-minute needs.

The organizers also work with artists in their community to design t-shirts and other materials. The march is used as a community fundraiser. The organizers also emphasize an ongoing commitment to the environment and stress the importance of keeping the places where participants organize free of litter.

Workshop

Make sure that the workshop presenters have the materials they need in advance. Does the venue have everything necessary for the workshop? If the presenters need a space to prep materials, such as assembling ingredients, do you have space where they can prep?

Dance

Make sure that the sound system works. How will you determine the playlist? Will there be a DJ, a playlist on a computer, or a band? How can you mix the music to fit the ebbs and flows of the crowd? Will there be rest areas? Will people have access to water?

Performances

Theater productions, dance performances, and recurring music performances are events that might happen eight or more times a week. For any recurring event, it is important to establish systems so you are not reinventing protocol each time. Keep materials in the same place and follow the same plan each time, unless you have to adjust when something is not working or something unplanned occurs.

Conventions and Trade Shows

Make sure you have a sufficient amount of tables. Make sure to check with the exhibitors and vendors about their electricity and space requirements in advance of the event. Some events require that vendors and exhibitors pay a fee to have a table—a possible fundraising strategy to offset costs for the event.

Outdoor Film Screening

Make sure you have a solid power source. If you are using an inflatable screen for an outdoor projection, make sure you have ropes and weights to tie it down in case of wind. You will need to secure film projection rights. It can be fun to have a pre-screening musical performance or speaker to introduce the film or films. Include subtitles if available to make the film more accessible. Film Noir au Canal, an outdoor film festival that happens in Montréal each summer by the Lachine Canal alternates between showing French-language and English-language films each Sunday. As Montréal is a multilingual city, during French-language films, the series projects English captions and vice versa in order to make the events more inclusive. Steps like these do not take long to implement but can expand the reach of the event and make it more welcoming.

Sports Match

In addition to making sure the facility meets all of the requirements of the sport, referees or officials have been secured, and teams have access to water, washrooms/bathroom/changing room facilities, there are ways to make a sports match more accessible for spectators. Sports can sometimes be hostile places for non-expert fans. Roller derby is notorious for its inclusive practices. At many roller derby matches, volunteers will hold "ask me about derby" signs and will explain rules to people who are attending a match for the first time. Actions such as this can bring in new fans and make the event feel accepting to people entering the space at all levels.

Conferences

If you are hosting a conference, there are several types to consider. See Part 3 for a detailed description of what to consider when hosting a conference.

PART 3: MULTIPLE EVENTS GROUPED TOGETHER: CONFERENCES/ CONVENTIONS

*C*onferences are larger events, often composed of several events. This section builds off of Part 2, giving particular attention to conference organization. However, I recommend that you also refer to Part 2 for information on technical details such as organizing hybrid events, discussions of language inclusivity, and publicity.

TYPES OF CONFERENCES

*T*here are several types of conferences: workshops, colloquiums, conference-conferences, conventions, and alternative conferences/unconferences. The main differences between conference types are the size and duration.

Terminology varies by region, field, and individual preference but there are some general differences, which I will detail in the pages to come.

Workshops

Typically workshops consist of a small group of people ranging from 5 to 30 participants focused on a specific goal. Workshops can be short or last several days. For example, a seed saving workshop would include workshop leaders who share information about the topic and participants who experiment with hands-on methods. Leaders might rotate throughout the day, with different participants leading mini-workshops within the larger workshop about specific topics.

Colloquiums

Colloquiums can be upwards of 50 participants and often consist of several panels or events around a related topic. The annual Feminist Research Colloquium I organize in Montréal creates a space for undergraduate and graduate students to share their ongoing research on gender, sexuality, feminist, and social justice studies with their peers, professors, friends, and larger community. Some folks would also call this a symposium—like I said, terms are flexible.

Conference-Conferences

Conference-conferences are often even larger and may welcome 40 to 2000+ people, gathering around either a related topic or a shared field or discipline. Conference-conferences center knowledge exchange, foster professional development, and dissemination of findings or practices. For two days, the Food, Feminism, and Fermentation Conference brought together scholars, journalists, artists, activists, farmers, chefs, cooks, baristas, brewers, authors, sommeliers, industry professionals, and curators all interested in the topic of feminist fermentation. The conference-conference format enables the sharing of information, networking, and socializing.

Conventions

Conventions are events organized around a specific industry, interest group, or fandom that provide a platform for enthusiasts to connect. Conventions tend to be larger events, with a greater emphasis on material or economic exchange. Zine conventions, small press conventions, and comic conventions often include presentations. Many conventions include a space where participants can have a table where they can exchange and/or sell their own publications and chat with other enthusiasts.

Alternative Conferences and Unconferences

There are also alternative conferences and unconferences. The DIY Methods Conference is a mostly screen-free, remote participation conference where attendees submit zines on their topics by a certain date to the conference organizers who then distribute the zines via mail and online. Alternative conferences experiment with format, timing, and how people can participate.

Unconferences are participant-oriented meetings where, usually during the event, attendees decide on the agenda, discussion topics, workshops, and even sometimes the time and venues. Any participant who wants to initiate a discussion on a topic can claim a time and a space in the unconference schedule. Other sessions are for open discussion. The idea behind unconferences is to focus on conversation over presentation. Unconferences, which tend to be smaller events, often are most fruitful when participants already have a high level of expertise or knowledge. For an unconference to be effective, there still needs to be a framework within which the experimentation can happen. While the scheduling of exact panels and discussions might happen on the day of the event, having a venue with accessible rooms, assistive technologies, and refreshments remains important. Organizers of unconferences can still make use of this book while developing the unconference infrastructure.

§

Remember, none of these definitions are hard and fast, but rather give a sense of the possibilities of scale. Workshops, colloquiums, conferences, conventions, and unconferences can occur in-person, virtually, or in hybrid format.

TYPES OF EVENTS AT CONFERENCES

*C*onferences consist of a variety of events. While every conference is unique, there are a few event formats that are common within conferences. Of course, be creative and make your conference your own!

Welcoming Remarks
Oftentimes, conference organizers welcome participants with some opening remarks. These statements often include a mix of

practical updates to the conference program; a series of thank-yous to collaborators, sponsors, grants, and other folks and institutions that made the conference possible; land acknowledgements; and some words about what the organizers hope participants take away from the conference. These remarks are sometimes followed by a keynote lecture; if this is the case, the organizers often read the bio of the keynote lecturer at the end of their remarks.

Keynote Lectures

Keynote lectures are typically around 45 minutes long, followed by a Q&A period. Some conferences have a keynote talk on the night before the conference begins or on the first morning of the conference. Typically keynotes are meant to set the tone for the event and bring all conference participants together. Oftentimes a leader in the field is invited to give the keynote address. It is typical for keynote speakers to be paid an honorarium ranging from hundreds of dollars to more than $2000. You might decide to have a group keynote, with several speakers, although this format is quite rare. You also might decide to forgo a keynote, instead emphasizing the various forms of knowledge all participants bring to the conference.

Panels

Panels often consist of three to four participants sharing papers or presentations for typically around 15 minutes each about a related topic. There is sometimes a panel chair who reads the presenters' bios and keeps track of the time. A Q&A period often follows the presentations. Panelists might share slideshows or other visual components. It is typical for panel events to last around 90 minutes, including the Q&A.

Roundtables

Roundtables typically consist of 3 to 5 participants chatting about a single topic. Rather than each participant sharing individual papers, projects, or presentations, usually a chair or panel lead has prepared a series of questions for the group to discuss, before opening up the discussion to audience Q&A.

Workshops

Workshops can take many forms. My preference is that workshops have an interactive component. The speaker or speakers share practical experience and then have activities for participants to try. For example, a podcast workshop might have participants experiment by making a short two to three minute podcast episode, practice cutting together audio on an open source audio editing platform such as Audacity, and coming together and sharing what they have made at the end of the workshop. Sometimes a workshop ends up looking more like a lecture. Depending on the topic and material workshops can range from one to five hours (or more).

Plenaries

Plenaries are sessions of the conference, such as a keynote, roundtable, or panel, that are designed for all conference participants to attend. Organizers do not schedule another event during the time of the plenary.

Poster Sessions

Some conferences have presenters share their work on posters that they then stand next to during a specific time period. Other participants can approach the presenters and ask them about their posters and work. These sessions can be useful for networking and for people to receive feedback about works in progress.

Performances

Performances at conferences can range from theater, dance, and music! Depending on what type of conference you are organizing, there might be many or no performances.

Exhibitor Halls

While some conferences have vendors, some conferences also have exhibition halls where participants can sit at tables and share or sell their work. Conventions often have exhibitor halls.

Meetings and Meetups

Perhaps there is a committee, subcommittee, affinity group, or other group that only has the chance to gather together at your conference. It is common for these groups to set up meeting times to talk about ongoing business, create gameplans for the future, and socialize.

Tours and Field Trips

Some conferences organize walking tours or field trips to offsite locations, with tie-ins to the conference theme. Some of these events might be organized by community partners.

Coffee Hours

Depending on the location of the conference, participants may not have other food options. Either organized by the conference, by community partners, or by sponsors, coffee hours can be spaces for people to network or socialize over coffee, tea, and light snacks.

Meal Times

Less traditional, but meal times are always key to the conferences I organize. While some conferences might provide food to participants, I like to integrate eating into the conference programming. I like to invite the caterers to speak about why and how they create their food and how that speaks to the conference theme. For the Food, Feminism, and Technology conference, my co-organizer Alanna Thain had the idea to have everyone drink their coffee together, with guided tasting, as the founder of the roastery and Dispatch Cafe Chrissy Durcak talked to us about her company's ethical approach to coffee. Throughout the conference, artist and chef Lisa Myers was cooking in the same room as conference workshops, panels, and roundtables, making the labor of the food preparation visible. Lisa then guided participants through our meal and as we ate, she explained her artistic practice and performed artwork about colonialism, blueberries, and residential schools. At the Oxford Food Symposium, participants eat all of their meals together and each day's opening remarks are followed by a presentation by the day's chefs explaining the significance of what we will be eating throughout the day. See the section in Part 2 on the role of food and alcohol to read more about how you can attend to different dietary restrictions, allergens, and more!

Parties and Celebrations

Conferences can include lots of kinds of parties and celebrations. People might celebrate a book launch with a wine and cheese event. Journals or publishers might host a time to mingle. The conference organizers might organize a dance at the conference venue or work with community partners to have after hours gatherings. Wherever these gatherings take place, make sure to include information about transportation, allergens, the presence of alcohol and/or other substances, and other accessibility information.

TIMELINE FOR ORGANIZING A CONFERENCE

*W*hile conferences can be organized in a shorter amount of time, below is a one-year timeline. I prefer to provide a less compacted schedule so that you feel like you can have fun planning the conference and can mitigate some of the stress that can come with conference organizing. The larger and more complicated the conference, the longer you will need to plan it.

Having a longer timeline does not only benefit you as a conference organizer. Sharing information in advance also provides people who might need to travel from out of town to attend the time to figure out their travel plans, arrange child or elder care, plan time off from work, and/ or make other arrangements.

As you organize your specific conference, you will be able to adapt this timeline to your specific needs. I have also provided templates and more details about each item in this book.

One Year (or More) Out

- ☐ Start to daydream: What do you want your conference to look like? What are the themes? Dream big!

- ☐ Begin to brainstorm practical details: See the brainstorming section in Part 1 of this book for directed brainstorming techniques.

- ☐ Look at what grants are available. What kinds of funding sources might you access? Grants are often on yearly or biyearly schedules, so make sure you find out deadlines far in advance.

- [ ] See if your town, city, or community has any grants or funds available to provide at least partial support.

- [ ] Begin to brainstorm potential sponsors.

- [ ] Determine whether it will be hybrid, in-person, virtual, alternative, or an unconference conference.

- [ ] Figure out if you have any start-up funds available. You might need funds to put a deposit on a venue or other rentals.

11 to 12 Months Out

- [ ] Figure out the venue/location. Book it as soon as you can.

- [ ] Figure out your dates.

- [ ] Determine if you need to apply for any kinds of permits or licenses.

- [ ] If you haven't started to apply for grants and want to, get on it!

11 Months Out

- [ ] Start to create a conference website with basic information on it, such as conference name, location, date, and a note about when more information will be forthcoming.

- [ ] Craft your CFPs (Call for Papers/Presentations/Panels/Workshops/Roundtables/Events/Performances).

- [ ] Design your form for presenter applications.

- [ ] Determine how you will decide which presenters are accepted and rejected.

- [ ] Determine if there will be a committee to go through the presenter applications (and then make the committee).

10 Months Out

- [ ] It is useful to have a rough sense of your budget and what conference fees will be at this point so you can share fee information with presenter applicants.

- [ ] Release your call for papers (CFP) and presenter application form at the same time (the link to the form should be included in the CFP). Make sure that these materials are available on your conference website.

- [ ] Begin advertising the CFP and your early conference website at this point. It is okay that you will have pages of the website that state "details to come." Share the CFP and website URL on listservs, social media, and even via flyers or posters if you mostly plan to involve folks who live locally.

- [ ] If you plan to have a conference keynote speaker or speakers, contact them now. Make sure to include information about any honorariums you may provide for their talk and if you are going to pay for their travel. Share your expectations about the length and format of the presentation.

9 Months Out

- [ ] Continue to advertise the CFP and conference website.

- [ ] You might be able to work with journalists to help get the word out! At the very least, you can start to build relationships with journalists now if press coverage of the event is useful.

- Are you interested in collaborating with other organizations or individuals to have conference adjacent events? For example, maybe you will provide programming from 9 to 5 each day of the conference but to encourage participants to visit other parts of the area or support local businesses in the city, you might have dinner, parties, dances, or even town tours held after 5. Start to make these arrangements.

8 Months Out

- Presenter applications are DUE. I usually give a 48-hour grace period for late applications, but you might decide to have a hard cutoff. Or if you do not receive enough applications, you can extend the deadline.

- Begin to read through presenter applications and rank the applications. The larger the conference, the longer reading through applications will take. You might consider doing this work within a committee.

- Decide what software you will use for conference registration. If you are charging for registration, you will need to pick a strategy for collecting fees and tracking payment. Determine with conference partners if they want to have separate ticketing for their events or part of the main conference registration form as an add-on.

6 to 7 Months Out

- Let presenter applicants know whether or not they were accepted, wait-listed, or rejected.

- Provide accepted presenters with a link to register for the conference first, especially if you have limited space capacity. Explain that the presenter must register by a certain date to confirm their participation.

☐ If you have a wait list, start to pull folks from the waitlist if others decline their offers.

5 to 6 Months Out

☐ Create the tentative presentation schedule. Put this schedule along with abstracts on the conference website.

☐ Write the announcement for conference registration. A few sentences describing the who, what, where, why, and how to register for the conference is key. You might create a visual component to accompany the announcement.

☐ Open registration for non-presenter participants.

☐ If you are hiring caterers, book them now! Especially if the caterers will be speaking at the conference (if this ties into the conference theme).

☐ Start to connect with journalists and media folks who might want to participate. It is typical to provide press passes.

☐ Update the conference website with information about where participants can stay if they are traveling from out-of-town and find accessibility resources. Optional: add a page with information about other nearby activities that may be of interest for visitors.

4 to 6 Months Out

☐ Create the conference program/booklet.

☐ Update the conference website with any new information.

- [ ] If you are having conference SWAG, start to design it and order it. If there are items that will be for sale, you can also have a preorder form or order link on your website.

- [ ] Monitor conference registrations. You might have to publicize the conference more or offer incentives for early registration. Or if spots are filling up quickly, share that information on listservs and social media.

- [ ] Set up meetings with potential vendors. Find out what they need (electricity, tables, space, etc).

- [ ] If there will be a bookseller interested in selling books written by conference presenters, connect authors with the bookseller.

2 to 3 Months Out

- [ ] Form your conference crew/volunteer team.

- [ ] Design conference t-shirt, hat, or uniform for the conference crew/volunteer team and order. These items can help participants identify the crew during the event.

- [ ] Ask presenters on roundtables, panels, and/or group presentations to plan to have slideshows or presentations within a single file, link, or on a single computer to reduce tech friction during the event.

- [ ] If speaker bios will be read and were not previously collected, make sure to connect presenters with the person reading the bios so they can be gathered in advance

- [ ] Continue to publicize the conference.

1 to 2 Months Out

- ☐ Print your conference booklet (if having printed programs/booklets).

- ☐ Continue to publicize the conference.

- ☐ You will likely receive lots of questions from presenters and attendees via email. In addition to responding to individual emails, update the conference website with information that might be of use for other participants.

- ☐ Follow up with your participants, vendors, and volunteers to make sure everyone is feeling set. It's useful to check in with folks.

- ☐ You will likely have some folks drop out and have to move some bits of the schedule around. This is normal.

Week Before the Conference

- ☐ Confirm details with your conference crew!

- ☐ Confirm details with the venue.

- ☐ Confirm final details with the caterers, including where to park.

- ☐ Send a reminder email to all participants with important conference details.

- ☐ Create directional signs to set up at the venue to guide people to conference locations, including all-gender washrooms.

- ☐ If your conference is virtual or hybrid and presenters have special panelist links, make sure they have their links.

Day Before the Conference

- ☐ Have a runthrough meeting with your conference crew/volunteer team.

- ☐ Set up all materials, tables, and tech that you can set up in advance.

- ☐ If you are able to have vendors' materials in a locked room, you can have vendors bring their materials the day before the conference so they don't have to arrive early.

- ☐ Send a reminder email to all participants with important conference details.

- ☐ If you are hosting a hybrid or virtual conference, send out the virtual meeting, virtual webinar, or livestream links. If presenters have their own panelist links, make sure presenters have their individual links.

- ☐ Confirm final details with the caterer for Day 1 of the conference.

- ☐ Send the reminder email to your conference crew/ volunteer team, including the shift schedule.

- ☐ Print out the crew schedule, your day-of checklist, conference schedules, and signs for the venue. Print off a list of your crew members' phone numbers in case you need to reach them. Print off a list of emergency contact numbers. Put these materials in your conference bag.

- ☐ If virtual or hybrid and presenters have special panelist links, re-email them their links.

- ☐ You will also likely receive lots of last minute questions via email. Be on top of your email today.

- [ ] Pack your bag for the next morning.
- [ ] Try to get a good night's sleep!

Day 1 of the Conference

- [ ] Send an early morning reminder email for participants.
- [ ] Arrive early. Try to arrive at least 90 minutes before the first participants arrive.
- [ ] Have your day-of checklist with the important micro details you will need to remember during the event.
- [ ] Check that the front door is unlocked and that signage near the front door and outside of the venue directs participants on how to enter the conference and find the check-in table.
- [ ] Unlock any rooms at the venue that are locked. You might have to call building security for assistance.
- [ ] Make sure that the sign in/registration table has all of the required materials.
- [ ] Make sure that some of the conference crew is seated at the welcome table and some of the crew is walking near the entrance to help participants locate the entrance.
- [ ] Be ready to greet the caterer and any vendors that arrive. Have conference crew members already allocated to help them set up.
- [ ] Make sure there is proper signage for the washrooms, including arrows pointing to the closest gender-neutral washrooms and water refill stations. If there aren't already tampons and pads in the washrooms, put out a basket with some freely available.

- [ ] Move the directional signs into the hallways so folks can find conference rooms. Post the schedules for each room on each room's door.

- [ ] Post the wifi code around the venue.

- [ ] Check that all of the volunteers on the first shift have arrived.

- [ ] Make sure the tech is ready in each room. You might do this with your conference crew and IT team.

- [ ] Have your phone volume on in case the caterer calls.

- [ ] If you are making introductory remarks, start on time to set a precedent for being on time for the rest of the day.

- [ ] If the first set of panels and workshops is supposed to start at a certain time, 15 minutes before the expected start time, plan to check in each room and check in with the room monitors that all of the tech is okay and that the presenters are finding their rooms.

- [ ] Have your device to check for last-minute emails. Check throughout the day.

- [ ] Rove throughout the conference, being available to answer questions or concerns from your team or participants.

- [ ] If you are running a hybrid conference, in addition to the role of the room monitors, jump into the different web streams, virtual meetings, or virtual meetings throughout the day to just check that the experience is going well for virtual participants.

- [ ] Check in at the front desk and see how check-in is going.

- [ ] Check in with your team again after the first time slot of the conference ends. During the 15-minute break between the panels, make sure the room monitors are all okay getting the next group of folks set up for their presentations.

- [ ] While you might be able to attend an event or two, you will likely need to be on-call throughout the event.

- [ ] Check in with the vendors to make sure their needs are being met.

- [ ] During the day, your role will be facilitating the conference. Make sure to network with conference participants, checking in on their needs and helping connect participants.

- [ ] Check with your conference crew that the bathrooms are clean and have enough toilet paper (have a crew member on top of this).

- [ ] If you haven't already done so, order lunch for the conference crew.

- [ ] If you are providing lunch for the participants, you will likely need to work with your food crew to greet the caterer 30 minutes to an hour in advance of lunch.

- [ ] Lunch time: make sure folks either are directed to the lunch area or that you have already provided participants with suggestions of nearby restaurants. If participants have brought their own lunch, direct them to where they can dine.

- [ ] If there is a midday break, it is a great time to check that the rooms are clean, the tech is running, and vendors are happy.

- [ ] If there are journalists attending, make sure to connect them with different participants who can speak about the conference. Make sure the journalists are receiving the resources that they need.

- [ ] Fifteen minutes before the next set of panels and workshops, you will again rove between the rooms and make sure everything is okay.

- [ ] Continue to check in on folks. You might actually get to watch some of the panels and presentations depending on how things are flowing.

- [ ] Again, 15 minutes before the next set of panels and workshops, you will rove between the rooms and make sure everything is okay.

- [ ] Continue to monitor the live stream feeds throughout the day.

- [ ] Continue to check in on the bathroom cleanliness.

- [ ] At the end of the day, participate in cleanup. Even if you have a conference crew, cleanup work is a shared effort!

- [ ] At the end of the day, touch base with your crew to see what went well and what could be improved for the next day/subsequent days.

- [ ] If there is an after-hours event, attend at least part of it to be supportive of your conference partners. If you can't attend yourself, try to have your conference co-organizer or at least members of your crew attend.

- [ ] Backup your photos of the event (and if someone is responsible for taking photos, ask them to do so too).

- [ ] Consider sharing some visual representation of Day 1 of the conference on social media.

- [ ] Prep the email you will send to all conference participants for the next morning.

- [ ] If you just have one conference shirt/uniform, wash it for the next day.

- [ ] Repack your conference bag for the next day.

- [ ] Rest!

Day 2+ of the Conference

- [ ] Repeat most of the sequence from Day 1. However, you will have a better sense of the flow.

- [ ] You might be able to attend more events on Day 2 if the conference is flowing well.

- [ ] If there is an after-hours celebration, again, try to attend.

Post-Conference (1 to 3 days after)

- [ ] You did it! Take a moment to acknowledge this giant accomplishment!

- [ ] If you didn't finish cleaning up the evening of the last conference day, finish cleaning up.

- [ ] Send a thank-you email/note to the conference crew/ volunteers.

- [ ] Send a thank-you email/note to the caterers. Make sure the caterer has received payment. If you need a receipt or invoice to get refunded from a grant or organization, make sure to collect it now.

- [ ] Send a thank-you email/note to the vendors.

- [ ] Send a thank-you email/note to conference partners.

- [ ] If you had keynote speakers, performers, or other folks you need to pay an honorarium, make sure to send the honoraria ASAP. You might need to follow up with these folks about documents such as tax forms, routing numbers, and other details.

- [ ] If working with journalists, you will likely have follow-up chats. Write them a thank-you email.

- [ ] Make a list of what went well and what mistakes you made. These moments are learning opportunities. Write them down while they are still fresh in your mind.

- [ ] Collect photos from your conference crew and/or participants.

- [ ] Share images from the conference on your conference social media/website and with participants.

- [ ] Rest!

Post-Conference (further out)

- [ ] Getting ready for the next one? Do you want to host another edition? Do you want to help someone else host another one? If you are hosting a yearly conference, you might start the cycle again quite soon after the end of this one.

- [ ] Publications? Some conferences lead to anthologies, collaborations, and a variety of publications. If you haven't already started to work on one, it is best to start working on it while the conference is still fresh in peoples' minds.

☐ If it is the first conference of its kind, how will you help folks stay in touch? Will you share email addresses? Create a directory? A listserv? Something else?

Every conference is unique, but this timeline provides a general sense of the tasks involved. The size of the conference will greatly impact your task list.

FORMAT/FLOW OF THE CONFERENCE

*C*onferences often mix and match a variety of events including roundtables, workshops, panels, keynotes, meetings, poster sessions, exhibitor halls, celebrations, and more. You may decide to have multiple streams of events happening simultaneously, which means participants will have options about what events they want to attend. You might decide to have a single-stream conference where only one event is happening at a time.

Decide if you will use what I will call a "block stream schedule." Within the block stream schedule, regardless of the format of event, each event is allocated 90 minutes.

Below is a simple block schedule that can include an unlimited number of streams. You might also add events that are outside of this block schedule such as tours, celebrations, exhibitor halls, and poster sessions. However, I find starting with this basic schedule to be a useful starting point.

A couple of notes:

Do not rush the break periods as they are pivotal for people to find the room for their next event, use the washroom, and socialize. This period is useful for the presenters during the next block to set up their tech.

The lunch break period will depend on how close your conference venue is to food options if you are not providing lunch. It is useful to provide participants with a map or list of nearby food options.

Day 1 Block Schedule Template

8:45-9:15: Welcoming remarks by conference organizers and breakfast (including a talk by the caterer if that makes sense for your event). (Some conferences might have a 90-minute block here so that there can also be a keynote)

9:15-9:30: Break

9:30-11:00: Block 1 (During this 90-minute period there will be either a single event if you are having a single-stream conference or multiple events.)

11:00-11:15: Break

11:15-12:45: Block 2

12:45-1:45: Lunch Break

1:45-3:15: Block 3 (Encourage presenters for Block 3 to arrive to their rooms 15 minutes early to set up their tech.)

3:15-3:30: Break

3:30-5:00: Block 4

After 5 PM you might have parties, celebrations, or collaborative events with community partners.

You might start some mornings later and might end the conference earlier on the last day. Format is up to you and the kinds of events you want to include. Be creative in your planning but make sure to provide participants with a clear schedule so that they can readily locate the events they want to attend.

COLLABORATIVE EVENTS

*C*ollaborative events with community partners can be a useful way to expand your programing without overextending yourself as an organizer. These events can also encourage conference participants to explore other parts of the town, city, or area where the conference is located.

As a conference organizer, I am prepared to schedule events from 9 to 5, but I like to collaborate with a community partner to organize mixers, tours, and other events outside of the conference hours. For the Queer Food Conference, we partnered with a local queer and feminist wine bar, Rebel Rebel and Wild Child of Somerville to have a wine and cheese event at their location. This event encouraged participants to explore more of the Greater Boston Area. The next night, we worked with Big Queer Food Fest to host their event after our conference wrapped up. Maybe you will have lunchtime events organized by community partners or pre-conference events that can welcome out-of-town attendees to the area.

Perhaps to build hype for your main conference you will host popup or virtual events in advance of the conference with other related organizations. For example, as part of our leadup to the Queer Food Conference, we co-hosted a virtual panel with the Oxford Food Symposium to highlight the work of queer food folks in Canada, the United States, and the UK.

Collaborative events facilitate networking. Work with your partners to determine ticketing, cost, and to discuss whether registration for these events will happen at the same time as the conference registration.

CALL FOR PAPERS/ PRESENTATIONS (CFP)

Y ou will need to circulate a CFP. The CFP has a few key pieces of information that you need to communicate.

• Short description of the conference: what is it? (two to three sentences)

- Where is the conference happening?

- When is it happening?

- What kinds of events will be happening (panels, workshops, roundtables, etc.)?

- What kinds of topics are you interested in having discussed at the conference? (one to three sentences)

- I like to share the conference registration cost on the CFP so people will know if they can afford to go/if it feels worth it for them. I am against requiring registration to apply to present as it creates unnecessary barriers and exclusion, though some conferences require membership fees to apply.

- Guidelines for submission (see below).

- Contact information in case people have any questions.

Below is a template of guidelines for submission that you can adapt for your own needs. This template is based on the CFP for the Queer Food Conference.

Template for Guidelines for Submission

Sessions will be _____ *(whatever length you decide works for your conference).*

Types of Sessions:

Panels of three to four papers with a chair/commentator: We strongly encourage the submission of full panels. You do NOT need to include someone to perform the chair and/or commentator role as part of your application (but you are welcome to include someone).

Roundtables, of four to five people (with a chair/commentator) who present, discuss, and interact with the audience on a single topic, theme, or issue. You do NOT need to include someone to perform the chair and/or comment role (but you are welcome to include someone).

Workshops with 1-3 leaders that center on an interactive and practical deep-dive into a subject. We will have use of a demonstration kitchen with two stove tops, a sink, a refrigerator, and monitors to project the action. Presenters will be responsible for bringing their own food materials, but we can supply cooking tools, tasting plates, and utensils. *(NOTE TO THE READER: Include whatever technical information you need to provide for workshops.)*

We encourage all full-panel and roundtable submissions to include a diversity of scholars and practitioners, including people at all levels of career development, from different institutions, and with different identities.

We will also consider individual paper submissions, out of which the program committee will assemble a very limited number of panels.

Finally, we will consider all-virtual panels, roundtables, and workshops. If your panel or roundtable is interested in presenting virtually, please indicate that as part of your submission. Please note that there are two different application forms: in-person and virtual.

Please only apply as part of one panel or paper submission. The exception to this rule is for the role of chair or commentator, which may be performed by someone who is also giving a paper or appearing on a roundtable.

All submissions are due by _____ *(date)*. The program committee will make decisions and send notifications by_____ *(date). (It is useful to tell people a date to expect decisions by to reduce the number of emails you receive asking you when folks will hear back. Overestimate the amount of time it will take.)*

Full panels and roundtables should include:

- Title of panel
- Panel abstract (200 words max.)
- Title and abstract for each paper (200 words max.)
- Biographical statement with contact information for each participant

Workshops should include:

- Title of the workshop or cooking demonstration
- Workshop or demo abstract (200 words max.)
- Abstract for each contribution (200 words max.)
- Biographical statement with contact information for each participant
- List of cooking tools required

Individual paper submissions should include:

- Title of paper
- Paper abstract (200 words max.)
- Biographical statement with contact information

Questions should be addressed to the _____ *(conference organizers' names and roles)* at _____ *(conference email address).*

Presenter Applications

You will need to have a system for collecting applications for presenters. Even if you intend to accept every application, having applications can help you design the schedule, help speakers prepare materials in advance, and provide you with important details such as contact information, accessibility needs, and more.

You might decide to have several application forms divided by the kinds of events or a single application form with multiple options.

Questions to ask include:

- ☐ Name

- ☐ Pronouns, if they wish to share

- ☐ Email address

- ☐ Other contact information you might require

- ☐ Name of paper/ workshop/roundtable (NOTE: If the application is for a full panel, make sure to also ask for the name of each individual paper/presentation within that panel)

- ☐ Abstract/description of paper/event (NOTE: Provide a word count. I recommend 100 to 175 words.)

- ☐ If you are organizing a hybrid conference, does the presenter want to be in-person or virtual, or are they open to either option?

- ☐ If you are allowing open-format events of different lengths, have the speaker explain the event and provide a justification for the length of the event.

- ☐ Technological needs? Projector? Sound/speakers? Other?

- ☐ Speaker bio: This bio can be shared later with the panel chair when the chair introduces the panel at the conference. Provide a word count. I recommend 50 to 125 words per person. If the person is applying with a full panel or workshop, you should provide a space for each speaker bio.

- ☐ Accessibility needs: Ask presenters to share their accessibility needs and also include a description of the accessibility features in place. It is important to know if the presenter cannot use stairs and half of the venue's rooms are upstairs; this way even if you cannot guarantee that every room at the venue is accessible, you can schedule their event in a room where stairs are not a barrier. If the speaker is only able to present if childcare is made available, knowing this in advance will give you time to accommodate this need.)

- ☐ If you are planning a hybrid conference, a question about how the presenter intends to involve in-person and online people equally. (Example: if they are distributing printed worksheets in-person, do they have a link they can share with online participants?)

- ☐ Affiliation (such as organization, institution, university, etc.) (required for certain grant agencies)

- ☐ A space for the applicant to share anything else they might need to share (such as a scheduling conflict)

I recommend using software such as a Google Form which will help you collect this information in an organized manner. Having people email you this information might mean that you miss submissions in a SPAM box.

A System For Determining Who Is Accepted

You might receive more applications than your conference can accommodate. It is useful to devise a system for choosing who to accept and reject ahead of releasing the CFP. Whether you are deciding alone or with a committee, write out your consideration factors in advance.

- Is it important to have a diversity of topics?

- Is it important to have a diversity of presenters with different identities (race, class, gender, sexual orientation, disability, age)?

- Is it important to have a diversity of different career levels (early career, students, experts, industry leaders)?

- Is it important to have a diversity of experiences (mixing scholars, journalists, people in industry, artists, activists)?

- Will you prioritize already formed panels or individual papers?

- If someone applies for both the in-person or virtual stream, how will you decide which stream to accept that person for?

- Will you create a waitlist in case any accepted presenters decline the offer?

- Will you offer poster sessions as an alternative?

- What counts as a good application? Detail? Topic? Something else?

- Will you suggest people team up if they have a similar topic?

I recommend having your conference committee use a color code system of green (yes), yellow (maybe), and red (no). Have the committee rank the applications. Discuss the greens, yellows, and reds separately. Make sure that you have also met your mandate for the factors you want to prioritize in acceptances.

Try making a sample schedule based on the acceptances to see how many people you can ultimately accept. If there are too many excellent proposals based on your plans, you might at this time decide to add an additional stream. Remember that there will be material constraints based on the physical space of the venue or the capabilities of your video chat/webinar platform for virtual or hybrid conferences.

You also need to decide if you are going to accept more people than you have places for, accept just the number of people you have places for, or waitlist people. The larger the conference, the more likely some people will reject their acceptance.

Communication with Presenters Before the Conference

There will be several times you will need to communicate with presenters before the start of the conference. The first time is when you inform applicants about the status of their applications (see the below templates). You will also likely need to follow up with the accepted presenters to remind them to register and confirm their participation. Anticipate that at least one person's acceptance or rejection email will end up in their SPAM box.

Template for Presenter Acceptance

Congratulations! Your proposal _____ (title) has been accepted for the _____ Conference taking place in _____ (location) from _____ (date). To confirm your participation in the conference, **we ask that you register for the conference by** _____ **(date and time).**

We plan to release the conference schedule _____ *(date)* and at that time, open up registration beyond accepted presenters.

Registration for the conference is $_____ *(cost)*. This registration fee covers 1) entrance to the conference, 2) a curated breakfast by local queer food businesses (with coffee and tea) on both Saturday and Sunday, and 3) *(whatever SWAG)*.

Please register here: _____ *(link)*

Then if you have other information to communicate, add it here _____.

We look forward to seeing you in _____ *(space of the conference)*!

Thanks!

The _____ Conference Organizing Committee

Template for Presenter Rejection

*T*hank you for your proposal to the _____ Conference. We received many proposals and unfortunately we are unable to accept your proposal.

However, there are still ways that you can participate in the conference. In _____ *(date)*, we will be opening up registration for the conference. We understand if you are not able to attend, but we hope we see you at the conference.

Thank you,

The _____ Conference Organizing Committee

Email Template to Share with Presenters the Week Before the Conference (and to resend the day before the conference)

This template is for a hybrid conference. This email can be useful for communicating important technical details. For a virtual-only or in-person-only event, you can still use this template; just remove the technical details that do not apply to your conference.

*D*ear presenters,

We look forward to your presentations during the _____ Conference.

The following email is long but it contains important information for the conference.

1) On the schedule *(provide a link)*, you will notice that there is a 15-minute break between panels/workshop/round-tables. Presenters, aim to arrive at your room *(whether it is the physical room for in-person presenters OR the Zoom room for virtual presenters)* at the start of the 15 minutes before your panel/workshop/roundtable starts. Doing so will enable your panel to connect to the room's tech and get set up for the live stream.

2) Every room will have a room monitor/tech monitor. This monitor will make sure that your panel/workshop/round-table is a) connected to the livestream, b) questions from virtual participants will be asked of in-person presenters AND questions from in-person participants will be asked of virtual presenters, and c) that the panel/workshop/roundtable ends on time. The monitor in the physical rooms will have a sign to indicate that the event needs to wrap up in 2 minutes. This monitor will be wearing a black shirt with the conference logo in purple font.

a) For virtual presenters, your livestream will be projected into a physical room at the conference.

b) For physical presenters, your livestream will be available for the virtual participants to watch.

c) We will not record the presentations.

d) We will distribute the Zoom links shortly before the start of the conference.

3) Each panel/workshop/roundtable is allocated 90 minutes. It is important to stay within the time limits of your event so that the next group of presenters can get set up.

a) If you have 4 panelists, we recommend that you plan for each panelist to speak for around 15 minutes and the remaining 30 minutes can be used for questions from the audience and discussion. Your panel can decide how you want to divide your time. *(Example: if you are 3 panelists, will you each speak for 20 minutes? Or will you have a longer discussion period? If you are 5 panelists, will you each speak for 12 minutes or each speak for 15 minutes with a shorter discussion period?)* We strongly recommend that your panel makes the decision this week so that each panelist can properly prepare.

b) If you have a roundtable, we recommend that your group decides on a group of questions that you will discuss in advance. You are also welcome to run your roundtable similarly to a panel.

4) There are no official panel/workshop/roundtable chairs. We strongly suggest that your panel/roundtable designates one person to timekeep and to read the presenters'

names and title of their papers. The names of everyone on your panel and their paper titles are available on the conference schedule.

    a) You all have access to each other's email addresses (in the CC of this email). However, if you have trouble contacting your fellow panelists, please let us know.

    b) There will be a set of physical time cards in the rooms for the time keeper to indicate how many minutes are left for each person's presentation.

5) PowerPoint/Google Slides: You will be able to display slides in the room. Plan to bring your own laptop and/or have a cloud version of your presentation.

It's not required, but we recommend that your entire panel/workshop puts your slides into a SINGLE Google Slides presentation. By having one slideshow, we do not have to spend time connecting and disconnecting from specific tech.

    a) You can import slides from PowerPoint, Canva, slideO, and other slide makers into a single slide show so that you can all have the aesthetics that you like.

    b) This step can save a lot of stress during the presentation period as connecting and disconnecting from tech can be frustrating. For virtual presenters, dealing with connecting and disconnecting from a screenshare can be annoying too.

We are so excited to see you!

The _____ Conference Organizing Team

YOUR TEAM

The People

Organizers

Are you organizing the conference alone? Are you working with multiple people?

If you are working with other people, I recommend being transparent about expectations and working with a few folks that you trust. Make sure to clearly designate your task lists. Organize regular check-in meetings and establish a system for communication. Be clear about when tasks will be completed, procedures for finishing tasks if someone has fallen behind, and how you would like to handle future disputes—during a period when everyone is feeling enthusiastic and happy to be working together. Clear and kind communication can make organizing the conference a much more positive experience.

Staff and Volunteers: Your Conference Crew

No one fully organizes a conference alone. Even if one person is in charge, a conference only exists through the efforts of everyone involved. Depending on the budget of the conference, the conference themes, and the organizers' capacity and network, you might pay people to work at the conference or have people volunteer to work shifts in exchange for free entry to the conference, meals, a t-shirt or uniform, and/or other forms of compensation for their time.

Write out a list of roles you'd like to have staffed. While it is tempting as an organizer to think you can handle everything, you will likely need to be handling things on a bigger scale and popping in and out to cover unanticipated challenges or details. It is useful to have folks designated to cover specific tasks so you can rove throughout the conference and allocate resources as needed.

Some typical conference crew/volunteer roles can include, but are not limited to . . .

- Sign-in table/check-in: distribute name tags, conference materials or SWAG bags, point people in the direction of rooms, and be there to answer questions.

- Greeters: direct people from front of the building to the sign-in table.[2]

- Room monitors: help presenters connect to the projector or other technology such as mics, amps/speakers, and the internet.[3]

- Food set-up: make sure food is arranged, signage identifying items and potential allergens are placed next to the dishes, and , plates, bowls, cutlery, and napkins are on the table.[4]

- Facility check-up: checks that rooms are clean and the bathrooms are properly stocked with toilet paper.

- Cleanup crew: Depending on the kinds of events that your conference includes, you might need to clean up between each event or just at the end of the day. As the conference organizer, while you will be partaking in all roles to various

---

2 If there's a central public transit drop-off point, bike parking lot, or car parking lot, you might want a crew member there to direct people to the sign-in table.

3 If you are hosting a hybrid conference, the room monitors will be especially useful. Monitors can ensure panels start and end on time. The busiest period for room monitors is the 15-minute period between events in the room when the monitor must help one set of presenters move out while the next group sets up their tech and/or materials.

4 If you are working with a caterer, it is useful for the food team to have the caterer's contact number. Ideally, schedule food to arrive at least 30 minutes before you serve it so that that food crew can do the set-up. This crew will likely also help move the trash, compost, and recycling out of the space after the meal ends (even if you are working with a venue with a cleaning staff).

degrees, I think it is important that you always partake in the cleanup.

- Photographer: As an organizer running around you might forget to document the event. Establishing one or two folks as the event photographers can ensure documentation of the event. Having photos can serve as useful memories and also can be useful to share with any sponsoring organizations or to share for future conferences and future sponsor and grant applications. It might not be appropriate to photograph certain conferences, so use your best judgment. You might also ask participants to indicate whether they consent to being photographed and sharing where these photos will be used.

Hybrid conferences require more staffing. To relieve the stress of the video stream dropping, I recommend that every room that is live streaming and every room with a live stream feed being projected into it has one room monitor. This monitor will make sure that the online and in-person folks are able to hear the audio and see the presenters. The monitor can assist with time keeping and tech set-up. Room monitors can also facilitate the question period, either reading questions aloud from virtual participants or sharing in-person questions with online presenters in case the audio quality of the initial question was insufficient. These room monitors are not the same as the IT crew.

The Logistics

Pre-Conference Meeting
While it might not always be possible, I recommend having a meeting with volunteers in advance of the start of the conference. Having this meeting and run-through the day before the conference can allow you to practice using the tech and make sure that

everyone is on the same page. After the run-through, I recommend sending every volunteer/crew member an email with reminders of what you covered. This email is useful to share in case anyone had to miss the meeting or forgot any details.

Make sure the crew knows who to contact and how to do so in case any problems arise.

Template: Volunteer/Crew Team Email Template After Run-Through/Day Before the Event

*V*olunteers,

It was lovely to do a run-through with you all today.

To recap what we discussed, I've included important technical details below:

Here is the schedule of your volunteer shifts: *(have a link to the spreadsheet with their shifts).*

If you are ill or unable to attend your volunteer shift, please let _____ *(organizer or head of volunteer crew team)* know right away.

If during the day something comes up, you can text _____ *(provide phone number of organizer or head of volunteer crew team).* Please text and don't call so I can attend to your message without disturbing the conference participants.

We will have free lunch for all of you on both days of the conference so you don't have to worry about getting lunch. Also, of course you can have the free breakfast too. *(Here is also where you can include information about a break room and/or a location with refreshments.)*

Also, feel free to attend any conference event when you aren't working a shift.

Please wear your conference t-shirt *(or whichever uniform you have decided on)* so that you can be identified as a staff member. For folks who missed the meeting today, we have your t-shirts.

For people setting up breakfast, working as a lobby greeter, or sitting at the registration table, please arrive at _____ *(or similar instructions for the first crew of volunteers)*.

For room monitors, make sure you are in the room 15 minutes BEFORE the panel/workshop starts. I have indicated that on the updated volunteer schedule.

Room Monitoring in Rooms with In-Person Events:

There will be a computer connected to the Zoom meeting in the room. In case the Zoom feed disconnects, we have created a Word document named "Links" saved on the desktop of each computer with the Zoom links on it. The computer log-in and password are written on the computer next to its keyboard.

You need to assist the presenters getting their slides onto that computer. We have asked them to show up 15 minutes before their panel/workshop begins so y'all can get the tech set up.

Presenters have been instructed to email their slides, create a virtual link, OR bring a USB stick. We also have a USB stick in each room that you can share with presenters to help them move slides off of their computers.

We know that some presenters might try to use their own computers but we've sent them an email about the policy of using the room computer as this will make the tech much easier for the day. Hopefully no one gives you too hard of a time about this.

Please bring your own computer, tablet, or phone to monitor the chat so that you can ask questions from the virtual attendees. It is useful to paste into the chat that attendees can ask questions via the chat that you will ask aloud during the Q&A period.

Each panel is responsible for their own time keeping. However, you need to make sure that the panel/Q&A session ends on time so that the next group of presenters can set up.

Room Monitoring in Room with Virtual Panel Being Projected into the Conference:

This room will project the virtual presenters' chats. You are responsible for making sure that the live stream is projected into the room.

Please bring your own computer, tablet, or phone to monitor the chat so that you can ask questions from the in-person attendees and share them with the virtual presenters. It is useful to let the in-person attendees know that you will be doing this. People in the room can also be logged into the Zoom webinar and type their own questions, just make sure that their volume is off so that there is no reverb.

_____ *(name of volunteer)*, you are roving taking photos. Please share them via *(link: DropBox, Google Drive, or whichever application you prefer)* after each day of the conference. If anyone else has photos they want to share, please also use these link: *(then share the link here)*.

Thank you!

_____ *(your name)*

T-Shirts/Uniform

It is useful to have some way for conference participants to identify the conference crew. A simple technique is to have a conference crew t-shirt, hat, or some other article of clothing that is easily identifiable, often with the name of the conference. Make sure that these items are distinct from the SWAG you distribute, even if it is just the color of the t-shirt so that participants can quickly distinguish who is a conference crew member. Distribute these items in advance of the start of the conference, often at the run-through meeting.

Shifts

I recommend having crew shifts divided into blocks, especially if you are running a block schedule for the conference. For example, if your morning period consists of a welcome period such as a breakfast with introductory remarks, Event 1 (such as a workshop or panel) for 90 minutes, a 15 minute break/ transition period, and Event 2 (such as another workshop, roundtable, or panel) for 90 minutes, you might assign a volunteer to cover the room monitoring shift from 15 minutes before Event 1 until the end of Event 2. This shift would be 3.5 hours and the volunteer would still be able to see 2 events, while assisting with the tech and time keeping. The rest of the day would be for that volunteer to use as they wish. They would be compensated with a free lunch. The next volunteer covering that room would arrive 15 minutes before the next block of 2, 90 minute events would begin.

You can communicate with your crew in advance about their availability, accessibility needs, and interests. If you have someone who is terrified of technology, having them monitor a live stream during a hybrid conference is probably going to just stress everyone out.

Let your volunteers tell you about their accessibility needs. Don't assume. For example, room or catering set-up might not be ideal for a crew member who is unable to lift heavy loads. Mobility disabilities might prevent a volunteer from leading a tour of the venue, but perhaps that volunteer would love to be at the check-in table.

When speaking with your crew about their availability, make sure to ask:

- What hours can they work?

- How long do they want to work? (You might have a minimum number of hours crew members must commit to, but some tasks might be shorter than others. By indicating length of tasks, crew members can also indicate what is possible for their accessibility needs.).

- What are their accessibility needs?

- What are their interests? Are there any tasks they are especially excited about?

- What do they want to avoid, if possible?

- Dietary requirements/restrictions/allergies?

- T-shirt or uniform size? (And if you have several options, what is their preferred design?)

Maintaining an Open Line of Communication

Try to maintain an open line of communication where your crew feels supported and comfortable to ask questions and share concerns. Asking about accessibility needs early on for all crew members can make participation available for parents, caregivers, people with different disabilities, and people who would like to participate but also have to balance other work responsibilities. We want to make sure that the conference is accessible for participants, but remember that your crew members are also participants. Let's take care of the people who are making the conference possible.

REGISTRATION

Y ou will need a system for participants to register for the conference. Even if you will allow day-of, walk-in registration, it is helpful to have advanced registration so you can prepare properly and anticipate the materials you will need.

There are a variety of platforms that can collect payment, collect contact information, and enable you to contact participants individually and as a group.

I recommend using a platform, such as Eventbrite or ThePointofSale.com, that includes multiple ticketing options. It can be useful to choose a platform that facilitates different registration periods for different groups of participants. For example, when you inform presenter applicants about their acceptance, I recommend requiring that they register to confirm their participation in the conference by a certain date. Having these confirmed acceptances means you can confirm your conference schedule and share it on your website when you open up the conference to general registration. You can also offer incentives for early registration by having a lower ticket cost if a participant registers by a certain date.

Hybrid Registration

Make sure that participants register for in-person or online participation. Your in-person event space will likely have a maximum occupancy that will limit the number of in-person participants. Depending on what software you use for virtual participants, you might have no participant limit or a very large number of virtual participants that you can include. On several registration platforms, you can limit the number of available tickets within each stream.

I recommend that you provide everyone who registers for in-person participation also with the links to the virtual conference stream to encourage people to stay home if they are ill. Providing these links to all registered participants enables folks to engage with the conference materials even if some unforeseen event occurs. Letting registered participants know in advance that everyone will get the online links whether they registered for in-person or online participation will also save you from having to answer a deluge of last-minute emails before and during the conference when your attention will need to focus on many other factors all at once.

Workaround Option

You can always have an online registration form and ask people to wire you money via PayPal, Interac, or a similar platform, send checks, or bring cash to the conference. However, you will have to keep track of a lot more details (and this is one of the benefit of these ticketing/events platforms).

Questions to have on the registration form and/or built into the registration platform:

- Name
- Pronouns (especially if you are printing out name tags)
- Email
- Phone number
- Accessibility Needs
- Dietary Restrictions/ Allergens
- If hybrid, in-person or virtual presentation

- If there is a sliding scale for ticket price, which option of ticket the participant needs

- What days does the participant plan to attend?

- If your conference has an on-site housing option, you might be able to have housing options included as part of the ticket options.

- If your conference has collaborative events with community partners with separate ticketing/separate cost, you might be able to have a check box option here

- Optional: Affiliation (if it is useful to know if someone is from a specific institution)

- If not already built into the platform, a link for the participant to pay for a ticket

- Any other information you need to collect

CONFERENCE WEBSITE

T highly recommend creating a conference website. The conference website serves to provide information to participants and potential participants. You can update it regularly with new information. There are a few key pages that should exist as part of your conference website. Below I explain what information is pivotal for each page.

What to Include

About Page

The About Page should answer the following questions: who, what, where, when, and why. Let readers know what the conference is. Tell readers where the conference is happening. Is it hybrid? Online only? In-person only? When is the conference happening? Where can people register to participate? Is there a final day to register? You can also include information about the background of the conference and the motivation for creating it.

Call for Papers/Presentations (CFP) Page

This page will have your CFP. Include a link to the submission page or include instructions for how people proposing presentations can submit. After the deadline for submission has passed, consider moving this page to a less prominent part of your website.

Registration Page

Even if you are using an external website for registration, the registration page should explain how participants can register for the conference and what dates registration closes. If participants must pay to attend the conference, you can explain pricing here, especially if there is a sliding scale. If you are providing housing that requires separate registration, indicate that on this page.

Contact Page

Have a page with contact information. I recommend setting up a conference email address to streamline all correspondence. You can forward this email address to your main email address to receive alerts, but retain the emails in the conference email account to have a record. Link to any social media accounts affiliated with the conference here.

Schedule Page

Here you can include a copy of the conference schedule. I recommend including a table with the different streams of the conference so participants can see what events are happening at the same time. Consider using color-coding within the table so participants can identify different kinds of events. For example, a blue background might indicate a performance whereas a green background may be a roundtable. Below the table, you can also include the abstracts of peoples' presentations and even speaker bios. You may decide to organize these by time slot or alphabetically. If you are printing a conference program, consider linking to a PDF version on this page.

Accessibility Page

Include information about location, bike parking, public transit and bike share programs, and car parking (including fees). Provide information about captioning, interpretation, and if your event is virtual or hybrid, the accessibility features of the online platform. Share information about where all-gender and wheelchair accessible bathrooms are located at the venue. Include the details about childcare, spaces to breast/chest feed, and chill-out spaces. Include information about health resources, such as COVID-19 precautions. (Will you have free masks available? Will you require masks to attend?). If you are providing food and/or drinks at the conference, explain what dietary requirements, allergens, and religious requirements are met. Here, you can also share information about the wifi access. This page can be a place to be transparent about the ticket price and why you have a certain price tag. You can also explain if there are any scholarships available to make participation more accessible.

Local Info Page

If you will have participants traveling to your conference from out of town, it can be useful to share information about other resources in the local area. For example, for the Queer Food Conference I shared information about the Boston public transit system and queer resources and businesses within the city. If you are providing housing options, share this information here (or on its own standalone page). If you are not providing housing, share information about local options here. I also used this page to highlight local queer businesses for when conference participants were looking for spaces to eat, drink, socialize, and shop nearby.

SWAG/Merch Page

If you are providing the option for participants to pre-order or purchase SWAG items such as conference t-shirts, hats, or other materials, you can design a SWAG/Merch page.

Optional: Additional Events

If your conference has partnered events, especially those with separate ticketing, it can be useful to have a web page sharing information about these events and linking to their registration pages.

Publications

If you are going to make a publication such as an anthology, collaborative zine, or edited collection after the conference, you might consider putting this information on your conference website before or after the conference. Include information about how people can submit their materials.

Anything Else You Need to Share with Your Participants

Add additional pages as necessary!

How to Build It

Even if you don't know how to code, there are a large range of website builders. I recommend, whether you are building your site from scratch or using a website-building company, you buy your own domain name separately so you can change hosts as you need. I build many websites on Blogger and GitHub, avoiding paying hosting fees and just buying a domain name. It is outside of the scope of this book to explain the step-by-step process of web design; however, even without prior experience, you can do it! You might also solicit the help of a friend with web design.

PUBLICITY/ADVERTISING FOR CONFERENCES

*T*here are several points you will need to publicize for your conference. You will need to share your call for papers/presentations (CFP). You will need to alert people when registration is open. If your conference is already affiliated with an organization, you might be able to just publicize the event on the organization's website, listserv, and social media. Consider sharing on related listservs, your personal social media, and social media accounts for the conference. Also encourage other people within your network to share your CFP and information about conference registration. Make use of your already established connections!

I recommend establishing social media accounts for the conference in addition to the conference website. Here you can share graphics and photos before, during, and after the conference. Creating this online presence is especially useful if you plan to have additional iterations of your conference or to release publications based on the conference preceedings.

While you may want to take photos during the event, designate someone on your conference crew to document the conference. Make sure to take a photo with your co-organizer(s), as you might forget while running around during the event. Create an online folder where your conference crew or even other participants can upload their photos.

For more information on publicity and advertising, see the Part 2 section on Publicity and Advertising. That section also contains important information about event aesthetics and design.

CONFERENCE PROGRAMS/ BOOKLETS ... AND GETTING CREATIVE

*P*rinting a conference program or booklet is not a requirement but can help make the conference more accessible to attendees without a smartphone. Obviously if your conference is virtual, having the schedule available on a website, in an email, or in virtual document can suffice. In-person attendees could scan QR codes spread around the venue linking them to the conference schedule. You can also print the schedule and tape it on walls around the venue and put each room's schedule on or next to that room's doors. (If doors are open, people might not be able to read the schedule if it is on the door.)

Printing a conference program or booklet can serve multiple purposes. It can serve as a practical document, political manifesto and/or a souvenir. Historically, conference programs have even led to massive protest, exciting discussions, and can represent the ethos of a conference. As Margaret Galvan discussed in her book *In Visible Archives*, the infamous 1982 Barnard Sex Conference's program was even censored! The program of the conference that is seen as pivotal in the feminist sex wars of the 1980s was more than just a schedule of events but included writings, art, and political commentary.

In advance of the Queer Food Conference, we collected recipes and headnotes with explanations of how participants thought their recipe reflected queer food. We printed *Cook Out! The Queer Food Conference Cookbook* which served as a conference program and a souvenir cookbook. The first few pages had the schedule, an introduction by my co-organizer and me, and the paper, roundtable, and workshop abstracts. The following pages had the recipes and headnotes from about one-third of our participants. I hired an illustrator (Amélie Ducharme) to design a beautiful cover and do the layout. In-person attendees got a physical copy for free and we made a PDF version of the cookbook freely available on the conference website.

I encourage you to think creatively! What kind of program would work for your conference? Depending on the quantity of programs you need, you can print quite a few copies at low cost. This program can mirror the design aesthetics of your conference logo, publicity materials, and website.

SWAG AND MERCH

*M*aybe you have gone to a conference before and gotten a cheap plastic object with the conference name emblazoned upon it. When I see these kinds of objects at a conference check-in desk, I imagine the object soon breaking and languishing in a landfill long past my own demise.

SWAG, however, can be done thoughtfully if tied into the theme of the conference and produced in a way that reflects the conference theme.

Does the SWAG have anything to do with your conference theme? For example, if you are hosting a queer wine producer conference are you providing a reusable wine glass that participants can use throughout the weekend and beyond?

How was the SWAG produced? Have you relied on exploitative sweatshop-produced materials or are you providing attendees with snack bags produced by local producers? Are the people making the goods being fairly compensated?

If you want to have t-shirts or other apparel, could you have an opt-in option so that attendees who would love a t-shirt can have the option to have one but that the cost isn't passed on to participants who have no interest in wearing it? Having a link on your website where participants can pre-order or order merchandise can help you print or build a certain amount of objects in advance without generating waste.

LODGING/HOUSING

*T*f you have people traveling from out of town to attend the conference, they will need a place to stay. Conferences held at universities or within hotels may have rooms available in the facility, sometimes at bulk discounted rates. Some universities make dorm rooms available for conference attendees during the summer or holiday breaks. Some hotels will enable conference organizers to reserve a block of rooms.

It is useful to provide information about housing options available for a range of budgets on your conference website. Some conferences even help connect attendees with local residents who have spare rooms or a couch, though this usually happens less formally due to liability issues that may arise.

CONFERENCE CHECK-IN/ SIGN-IN/WELCOME TABLE

*T*t is important to indicate to conference participants in advance of the conference start where they can sign in, find necessary information, and be welcomed to the conference. If a conference is happening in a single building, having the check-in table near the front entrance can make it easy for people to find. If you are hosting the conference on a large campus, around a city, or on rural lands, make sure that participants have the coordinates of this table so they can navigate to it readily.

The role of the conference check-in/sign-in table is multifold. This table is where participants can announce that they have arrived. They can gather or make their name tags. They can pick up conference materials such as a conference program, SWAG, meal tickets, or any other materials you need to give them. If your conference includes housing, decide if participants will pick up their room keys here or at another location near the residences. This table also serves as a de facto information table where participants may request directions, share concerns, or ask any other questions.

It is useful to have the most amount of volunteers on the first morning of the conference, if you are having a multi-day conference. However, there should always be one person at the table as participants might arrive late, only attend part of the conference, or also just want a place where they can find information.

What to have at the table:

- List of participants—have multiple copies. If your conference is larger than 50 participants and you expect everyone to arrive around the same time to the table, you might divide the list into different sections of the alphabet. For example, A through K last names go in one line to check in and L through Z in the other line, or something like that. Either way, make sure that the volunteers at the table have multiple copies of the participant list.

- Pens and markers to check names off the list.

- Name tags. You can either print name tags in advance or have attendees make their own. I am a fan of having participants write their own names and pronouns. You can either print name tags in advance or have attendees make their own. I am a fan of having participants write their own names and pronouns. If you are using name tags with lanyards, you might consider providing different color options for the lanyards to indicate participants' comfort with different kinds of greetings. A green lanyard may indicate "comfortable with handshakes, potentially hugs, and more physical greetings." A red lanyard may indicate "I prefer to keep physical distance," and a yellow lanyard may indicate "potentially open to handshakes and physical greetings." If you use a lanyard color system, make sure to provide attendees with information about their meaning through signage at the check-in table.

- Conference programs and conference schedules. Have you printed a program? Give it to folks when they sign in. Even if the schedule is only available for participants on the conference website, it is useful to have a QR code near the check-in table so participants can readily find the schedule. It can also be useful to print out a copy of the schedule and have it near the check-in desk so volunteers can readily answer questions about upcoming events and locations. Having a couple of printed copies can also make the conference more accessible for participants without smartphones.

- Cash box or way to digitally accept payments: if your conference allows walk-ins and has a participation fee, you will need a way to collect money. There are lots of different apps for collecting money via phone. Some participants may want to pay in cash, so it is useful to indicate whether or not cash, card, or e-payment will be accepted.

- Volunteer schedule/task list: it is useful to have a copy of the volunteer schedule so volunteers have a place they can quickly check without needing their phone or other device.

- Room keys and SWAG are often distributed at this location.

- Masks for participants are also often distributed here.

- Construction tape (so it doesn't damage wall paint), blank white paper, and markers in case you need to make any last minute signage.

- Lost and found box—even if you have another lost and found location, it is likely participants will bring and/or search for objects at the check-in table.

- Emergency contact numbers, including facility numbers. Is there a leak and you need to let the venue know? Is someone having a health crisis? Providing volunteers with a plan of who to contact in advance is useful, but having a document with these numbers at the sign-in desk can empower your team to handle a crisis or challenge.

END-OF-DAY REFLECTION

*A*t the end of the day reflect on what went well, what could be improved, and your gameplan for the next day (if you have a multi-day conference). You can also use a version of this worksheet after the conference concludes. It is best to write down reflections when the conference is still fresh in your mind. You can go over this list with your conference crew to solicit their feedback during the end-of-day meeting check-in period.

- What went well today?

- What did not go as planned?

- What could be improved with the technology/IT?

- What could be improved with the conference crew?

- Did any crew members have suggestions or complaints?

- Did any participants have suggestions or complaints?

- Is there anything else that can be improved?

- What will you do differently tomorrow?

- Do you need to communicate this new plan with your conference crew?

- If so, have you communicated this new plan yet?

PUBLICATIONS

*D*uring your conference, participants will share ideas, make intellectual and social connections, and may be inspired to collaborate on a post-conference project. Sometimes publications inspired by conferences are the result of this post-conference excitement.

While conference participants may use the event as a space to do their own networking, decide to collaborate on projects, and/or decide to co-write pieces together. As a conference organizer, you might decide to create official post-conference publications such as an anthology, an edited collection, or a less formal zine. As post-conference publications are not rare, you might already anticipate or plan for a publication as part of your conference planning process or you might be so inspired by the conference that you will decide to edit or organize a publication after the conference wraps up. Although a full guide on publishing an anthology or edited collection is outside the scope of this book, there are a few factors you will need to consider.

How will you decide who to include in the anthology, edited collection, zine, or other post-conference publication? Will you issue an invitation to all participants to submit ideas or completed pieces for the publication or will you approach specific participants to submit? What will your parameters for publication be? Do you have a specific length and format in mind? Will the volume include a mix of art, poetry, essays, drawings, recipes, or other materials? Will it be a collection of essays? Will you invite every participant to share post-conference reflections? Will you open the publication process up to people who were not able to attend the conference but work on related topics, issuing either personal invitations or distributing a public CFP (call for papers)? Determining your format and specifications for submissions in advance is useful as you can communicate this information to potential contributors.

Once you decide how you will elicit contributions, it is important to request either abstracts or full contributions soon after the end of the conference. You want to make sure that the ideas generated during the conference are still fresh in your participants' minds. While it is important to give yourself some time to rest after organizing a conference, you want to also make sure to reach people before they have moved on.

How would you like to publish the book or zine? Will you self-publish an e-book, hosted on your conference website? Will you self-publish a printed book? Will you collect contributions on a Google Doc or similarly shared document and paste them into a zine, before photocopying them? Or will you seek a traditional publisher? Depending on the kind of press you hope to work with, you might have to acquire a book agent as many presses do not work with unrepresented authors and editors. Agents may host a book auction or reach out to specific publishers. Working with a press usually involves writing a book proposal and including sample chapters. Every publisher has their own strengths and weaknesses so it is important to know what your goal with the project is in advance.

Money is an ongoing discussion with book and zine publishing. Do you intend to pay contributors? If so, how? While some folks intend to equally split profits of a book, this might result in folks receiving only a few dollars or cents each. It is possible to write grants to try to support a publication, as I did with the Queer Food Conference, so that you can pay people for their labor. If the publication makes any money after printing costs, how will you distribute funds? Will money go to future iterations of the conference or towards a community organization? Will you as the editor or organizer receive the funds to compensate you for your work? It is important to be transparent with contributors about the financial aspects of the publication. At a minimum, try to make sure that every contributor gets at least one free copy of the publication to compensate them for their work.

Publications are a great way to continue the conversation from the conference and include other people who were not able to participate in the original event. Before the release of the book or zine, make sure to promote the publication on your social media accounts, on your website, and with the network of journalists you established in the original publicity campaign for your conference.

WRAPPING UP

*W*ow! You did it. You hosted a conference. Whether it lasted for one day or many days, organizing a conference can be a very rewarding and intense experience. There are initial tasks you have to do at the conclusion of a conference, but the first step is to take a moment to pause and realize your success. It is important to acknowledge what you have accomplished before moving on to the next steps. Great work!

Initial Post Conference Wrap-Up
In the initial post-conference period, you will have a series of small tasks to complete. You might have some cleanup to finish or need to return rentals or other equipment. Make sure to send thank you emails or notes to your conference crew, volunteers, vendors, and conference partners. In addition to thanking them, make sure the caterer has received payment. If you need a receipt or invoice to get refunded from a grant or organization, make sure to collect it now. If you invited keynote speakers, performers, or other folks you need to pay an honorarium, make sure to send the honoraria as soon as possible if you did not pay them in advance. You might need to follow up with these folks about documents such as tax forms, routing numbers, and other details. If you have been working with journalists who are covering the conference, you will likely have follow-up chats. Whether or not the conference makes the news, write them a thank you email for their time and consideration.

The initial post-conference period is a useful time for reflecting on the conference while details are still fresh in your mind. Below is a list to help you evaluate what went well and what mistakes you made. These moments are learning opportunities. Write them down while they are still fresh in your mind.

- What went well during the conference?

- What were the highlights?

- What were your favorite moments?

- What did not go as planned?

- What were the low points?

- What could be improved with the technology/IT for the future?

- Were there ways that the conference could have been more accessible?

- What could be improved with the conference crew?

- Did any crew member have suggestions or complaints?

- Did you effectively communicate with the conference crew before, during, and after the conference?

- Did any participants have suggestions or complaints?

- Did you effectively communicate with the participants before, during, and after the conference?

- Is there anything else that can be improved?

- If hosting the conference again, what would you do differently?

- How are you feeling?

In the days shortly after the conclusion of the conference, you will also want to collect photos from your conference crew and/

or participants. You can set up a DropBox, Google Drive, or other photo sharing account. If you shared a hashtag with conference participants, look at the posts that utilized this hashtag to see what participants were sharing. Share images from the conference on your conference social media, on your website, and with participants.

After the bills are paid, the materials are returned, and you have sent the wrap up emails, take some time to rest and celebrate.

Next Steps

A few days or weeks have passed and you have caught up on sleep and enjoyed your success. Now you can begin to think about the next steps.

It is likely that if people had a great time at the conference they will start talking about the next one. Folks who were unable to attend this conference also will start to message you asking about the next iteration of the conference and trying to learn when and where the next one will be. It can be really exciting to receive this kind of feedback, but it might also be overwhelming as you are just starting to recover from the last one. Be honest with yourself if you want to host another edition. You might consider helping someone else host another one or you might be comfortable with the conference being a one-off event. If you are hosting a yearly conference, often as part of an organization, you might already have a sense of the next location and date. Yearly conferences often mean that you will start the organizing cycle again quite soon after the end of this one. Some conferences are on biannual or triannual cycles. Find what works best for you and your community!

The post-conference period is also when you will start working on publications. It might be more sustainable to host a conference one year and the next year focus on a publication before hosting the next edition of the conference the following year.

If your conference was the first of its kind, how will you help folks stay in touch? Will you share email addresses between participants? Create a directory? A listserv? Something else? Will you establish an association or a more formal organization? If you are interested in hosting a recurring conference and will continue to seek grant and community funding to financially support the endeavor, you might consider founding an association and seeking non-profit status which may make you eligible for certain grants. Once you have evaluated your funding options and seen what the requirements are for grants, it may or may not make sense for you to formalize your conference organization.

PART 4: ORGANIZER NEEDS

Organizing an event requires time, energy, and can be very emotional. With every event, you will learn new skills and techniques. As you continue to organize events, you will develop your own systems that will assist with your organization. As an organizer there are practical things to keep in mind, but it is also important to care for the wellbeing of you and those around you.

IN YOUR BAG

L et's start with the practical. No matter the event, I recommend that there are a few things you have in your bag.

Emergency Signage Materials

Always have tape, scissors, paper, and a bold marker on you. Ideally you have both masking tape and duct tape. You never know if you will need to make a sign with arrows to direct people where to go. Masking tape won't rip paint off of walls. Duct tape has a wide variety of applications. Markers, pens, and paper are useful if—shocker—you need to write anything down.

You will want to have clear and visible signs for accessible entrances, parking, washrooms, public phones, transit points, and other conveniences.

Key Documents

Carry printouts of the schedule, emergency numbers, your to-do lists, and your volunteer/crew contact info. Have back-up copies of the attendee/ participant list. Have a map of the venue close at hand to direct lost participants.

Cash

If there is something that needs to be bought at the last minute, it is helpful to have cash in case you can't personally run out and get it but need to send a friend, volunteer, or crew member. It is easier to hand over cash than a credit card. Ask that person to get a receipt though if you are hoping to get reimbursed from organizational funds or grants.

Tech Items

If there is any tech involved in the event at all, bring chargers, cords, USB sticks, connector cables, a laptop, and a phone. I live in Canada and just from walking to a venue, the winter cold can kill my phone battery. Oftentimes, presenters and performers and I plan to contact one another by texting before an event. To have a dead phone battery can increase stress unnecessarily. Having back-up computer chargers, batteries, extension cords, and USB sticks can be game changers. I often hold events in rooms where I haven't been able to try the tech before. I bring my own computer, connector cables (such as USB to VGA or USB to HDMI), and USB sticks just in case a computer doesn't work with the tech set-up of the venue. Even though you ideally will have done a tech run-through in advance, be prepared and have a back-up plan.

I also want to make sure I can attend to any last minute detail as an organizer so having my phone and laptop with me at all times can enable me to do so. Remember, it is likely that people will be emailing you with last-minute questions.

Self-Care Items

Bring a water bottle and snacks. Make sure to hydrate and attend to your bodily needs. Keep snacks on you! And if the event is outside . . . sunscreen, a hat, and sunglasses!

SELF-CARE

O rganizing events and conferences can be extremely gratifying experiences. Of all of the work I do, I find event organization one of the most fulfilling. Bringing people together to share ideas, connect, and network brings me so much joy. When an event flows smoothly, I feel a mix of emotions. On the one hand, I feel pride for a successful event. However, I also tend to feel relief and can finally exhale after the build-up of anticipation and stress.

Organizing events requires you to think through countless details, juggle multiple commitments simultaneously, and balance the needs of participants, the organizing crew, and your own personal needs. While I hope that this book's checklists, templates, and guides empower you to feel prepared for your events, organizing brings up a lot of emotions.

Tips

Here are a few tips that have helped me care for myself while organizing last minute gatherings to international hybrid conferences for hundreds of people that I started working on 14 months in advance.

- Advance planning: If I can give myself plenty of time to plan, I have time to adjust to the ebbs and flows of life. I can also have more flexibility to adapt. While sometimes you need to organize an event last minute, ideally you will be able to give yourself plenty of time to plan.

- Systems: I have developed a series of systems, shared throughout this book that make organizing events more feasible. With the Disrupting Disruptions speaker series, I am often hosting one or two hybrid events per week. Rather than reinvent my process each time, I have developed a system that saves time. I created a template invitation email that I only have to update for each speaker. I use the same platforms for event registration (though I had to adjust when folks stopped using Facebook Events as much, and I also had to adjust when the COVID-19 pandemic meant shifting everything to online events). I hire dependable folks that I trained to help with the event recording and upload to our series YouTube channel. I hire CART captioners through the same service. We use the same paperwork to process speakers' honorariums. I use the same social media accounts to promote the event. And so on.

Developing dependable systems relieves a lot of stress. While you may still need to balance numerous details, you know that you have systems you can count on that have worked for you before. I hope that you are able to take advantage of the systems and templates I shared in this book and adapt them for your own needs and context.

- Surround yourself with dependable people: Even if you are organizing the event alone, you will likely be collaborating with people on one or more components of the event. Working with people you can depend on is so valuable. I am fortunate to be able to work with people who I know will show up when they say they will and follow through on their tasks. Of course, life happens and it is important to have grace and compassion for the people we work with—all of us are never our best selves all the time—but being able to depend on reliable people makes organizing much more sustainable.

- Keeping perspective: Sometimes things don't go perfectly well. Sometimes a glitch or hiccup, even if it is completely outside of your control, can feel embarrassing, frustrating, or upsetting. For the speaker series, I have committed to always have CART captioning for virtual or hybrid events. One time I was hosting an event in which I knew we had participants attending who specifically told me that they needed the captions to be able to fully participate.

This event was with a popular speaker and over five hundred people had registered to attend, adding an additional level of excitement and stress. Of course, the day of this event was the only time in the history of the series when the captioner did not arrive on time and we had to re-launch the Zoom webinar to try to get auto-captions to begin while we awaited the arrival of the captioner. When the captioner arrived (only actually a few minutes late), I had to try to end the auto-captions so there were not double captions, all while introducing the speaker to the hundreds of attendees. Let's just say that during those few minutes, I ended up drenched in sweat, was worried I seemed very unprofessional, and just felt terrible.

The most important thing was that the people who needed captions had access to the event, and I am glad that even with our glitch, I was able to facilitate that. However, I just felt terrible. In the follow-up to the event when I reached out to people who registered with the recording link I, of course, apologized about the caption issue for the first few minutes. The thing is, people understood that these things happen. I used the moment to adjust my systems for com-municating in advance with the captioners and now send an additional reminder email before each event I host. I used the incident as a learning experience. In the grand scheme of things, this is a small thing, but I was lucky to be surrounded by friends and family (and my fantastic dog) that help me keep perspective. Learn, grow, and continue to do the work!

- Celebrate the wins: Writing grants for funding, booking venues, inviting performers, booking caterers, connecting with community organizations and vendors, publicizing the event, and handling all of the details means that it is easy to get lost in the details of hosting an event, series, conference, or convention. When something good happens, take the time to pause and celebrate it. Did you win a grant to support your event? Woohooo! Congratulations! Take some time to mark this occasion. Did the musician you hoped to play agree to be part of your festival? Do a happy dance (or whatever you like to do)!

- Rest: When you decide to take a break, take the break. Do not feel guilty about not working. Do not ruin your break by worrying about work. Let yourself rest. It is important to give yourself time to pause and relax. Do things you enjoy.

- Gratitude: Take the time to tell the people you are working with that you are grateful for their contributions. Gratitude also encourages a better working environment that is most fulfilling and rewarding for everyone involved.

NAVIGATING SUCCESS AND FAILURE

Defining Success

How will you determine if your event was successful? Attendance? Sales? People telling you after the event that they had a fun time? Participants sharing they learned new skills? Something else? It can be useful to determine what success means to you before the event so that you also do not hold yourself to a level of unattainable perfection. You have undertaken a huge task, which is a brave endeavor. There is always room for improvement, but it is already amazing that you have organized this event.

Mistakes

No matter how well you have planned your conference, mistakes and mishaps will happen. Post-conference recaps with your conference crew are key after each day to make sure everyone is on the same page for subsequent days. Give yourself time to reflect on what worked and what did not. Be open to feedback from participants. These moments are growing opportunities that will help you organize subsequent events.

Failures and Disappointments

Sometimes you host an event and no one attends. Or what if the speaker just does not show up? Or what if you have planned an outdoor sunflower festival and a blizzard comes to town one hour before? Or there is a power outage and now you can't host the online guided meditation and poetry reading? Or you ran out of food at the food festival?

Some of these problems are caused by things that would be completely out of your control. You can't control the weather. You can make contingency plans, rent tents, and make rain plans, but even still some of the event planning is just luck: good or bad. There are other circumstances that maybe you underestimate the number of attendees or overestimate the amount of people who would want lemonade, and now you are left with vats of lemonade and lost money on the event.

After feeling your feelings, take the time to evaluate what happened and what you can do for the future. In the case of the lemonade event, see where you can improve registration. Maybe people have to pre-pay for their lemonade when they register so even if they don't attend you haven't lost money and can just sell extra, give it away, or donate it. Improve your publicity strategy, and evaluate if maybe a curated, artisanal lemonade event is even what you want to host.

Perspective

We can plan, make contingencies, use our community networks, and think through every detail of the event. We can set ourselves up for success. However, sometimes success is also due to luck.

One of my favorite events I ever hosted also was a success due to luck. When my book *Ingredients for Revolution* came out, I wanted to do a variety of book launch events. While I love speaking at independent bookstores, giving talks at libraries, and doing formal lectures at universities, since my book on lesbian and queer women's feminist restaurant history also involved a history of the women's music movement, feminist parties, and social gatherings, I wanted to host another kind of book launch.

Each year I volunteer at Montréal's Rock Camp for Girls, Non-Binary, and Trans Youth, where campers get together to learn and make music for empowerment and community building. Through volunteering there, I have met so many awesome queer musicians. I decided to make my book launch a Historical Queer Music Night that served as a fundraiser for Rock Camp.

On a Monday night in January 2023, over 90 people showed up to Turbo Haüs Bar to hear me talk about queer feminist history. I introduced the event and gave a bit of context about the event, invited some of the leaders of Rock Camp to say a few words, then one of my friends performed a short, 3-song cover set of the queer musician Phranc. After her set, I then talked more about the connection of feminist restaurant history and queer women's music history and read a few pages of my book aloud, while the next performer got ready for her set. This friend played a cover set of Beth Elliott, an amazing trans lesbian musician, and told the audience about Elliott's musical contributions. Next, I invited one of my students to speak about her research on Montréal's queer music history while the final performers, a band planning to cover Joan Jett's music, tuned their guitars.

After the final set, we announced that we raised over $900, which covered the full scholarships for at least 3 campers. My book editor sat in the corner selling my book and zines alongside Rock Camp shirts and the performers' CDs. Yes, I had made use of my community networks and shared the event on listservs, social media, and flyers. The participating musicians, speakers, venue, and even my book's press also shared news of the event within their networks. The venue, which is known in Montréal for supporting artists, let me use the space for free as it was a community fundraiser. It was a pay what you can, but $10-suggested fundraiser, which made the event financially accessible to the demographic audience. However, it was still an event held in Montréal on a Monday night in January. Where was the luck?

Well while -40 C (same as -40 F) is not uncommon in January in Montréal, this Monday night was a balmy -2 C or 28 F. This warm weather meant many attendees did not even wear jackets when they walked, biked, bused, or metro-ed to the venue. People were excited that they could be outside without the air hurting their face. The lack of other events that night in the city meant that my event was not competing with something more exciting. Sidewalks had already been cleared of the snowstorm from days before. And the sky was clear—no snow, rain, hail, or wintery mix. While I may have planned well and my musician friends are extremely talented, had it not been for the lucky weather, there is no way the event would have been such a success.

I bring up this story for a few reasons. One is because this event demonstrates ways that you can reimagine what an event can be. A book launch can be a musical performance with readings and act as a fundraiser that uplifts various folks in your community. You can have fun with your event organizing! This event was also only possible due to having amazing community support. Let's take care of the people around us as doing so will help us all succeed. I also again want to underline that there is always a bit of chance when doing this work. A wire might break, but a venue might also have a particular date available last minute. Being an event organizer means that you will try to control what you can but will also have to accept and adapt to the things you cannot.

WHEN TO STOP: NAVIGATING ENDINGS

*H*ow do you know when to stop a speaker series or conference series? If you are hosting a one-off event, there is a logical conclusion to your event because it will end. However, if you are hosting your event as part of an ongoing series, how will you know when to wrap things up? Sometimes running out of funding, time, energy, or interest leads to a logical conclusion. I have been running the Disrupting Disruptions speaker and workshop series since 2019. I told myself that when the funding ran out from my fourth major grant and after 100 events, I would no longer regularly host events. Due to funding and scheduling, I ultimately organized 106 for the series.

I know that hosting the occasional event with a community partner will continue to publicize the collection of video recordings of the past events on the website and will help connect people with the resources I curated over the past five-plus years. However, while it has been a great honor to bring so many people together around these topics, when hosting started to feel like more and more of a burden and less fun, I knew it was time to start to wrap up the series. Letting go can be really hard.

Consider checking in with yourself from time to time and ask the following questions:

- Has my series accomplished what I set out to do?
- Do subsequent events or conferences seem to be getting better or worse?
- Is there still interest from audiences?
- How is attendance?
- Am I still enjoying doing this work?
- Do I still have the funding and resources to continue doing this work?
- Do I want to continue doing this work?
- If I am afraid about ending the series, what exactly am I afraid of?
- If there are parts that I want to continue, have I set up infrastructure to enable the continuation of these components? If not, can I?

It can be hard to know when to end things though, and sometimes rather than finishing something completely, you can pass it on.

It's Never Really Over: Passing It On

It is important to share your knowledge with others. Mentor and train other people with the skillsets you have picked up while organizing events and conferences. If you are organizing a recurring event, conference, or speaker series, you can pass on the organization to someone else who you may have trained as part of your work organizing the events.

Document what your processes are. Write down your systems. If you have found particular vendors, caterers, vendors, community partners, and other folks to be great to work with, assemble their contact information into one place. If there are website logins, social media accounts, passwords, grant financial information, banking information, and other pertinent information for anyone organizing the series or conference, assemble it together. You might create a folder in the cloud or make an information binder. Assembling this information as you organize your series might not seem the most important at the time, but if you plan to pass on the series, conference, or convention, it is useful to be able to direct the next organizers to a single resource that will answer any questions they may have.

It can be difficult to pass on the reins as people will have their individual approaches, but passing on the series or conference can lead to new, creative ideas and will let the event evolve. The event, series, or conference will likely be different and that is okay.

CONCLUSION AND ACKNOWLEDGMENTS

*D*ear readers, after reading this guidebook, I hope you are inspired to organize inclusive events and conferences! I hope you can benefit from the process of my learning from my mistakes.

This book would not be possible without the body of feminist and social justice literature that continues to shape me and my work.

Thank you to the writers, thinkers, activists, and artists who inspire and challenge me. Thank you to the activists in the disability rights movement who continually bring awareness to the importance of accessibility.

Thank you to everyone who has ever attended an event or supported a conference that I have organized. Thank you for your patience as I learned what worked or did not work. Thank you to every group and individual with whom I have had the pleasure to collaborate.

Thank you to the amazing team at Microcosm for believing in me. Thank you to Joe Biel, Elly Blue, Olivia Rollins, and Ivy Zeller.

Thank you to Alanna Thain, Maya Hey, and Megan J. Elias for co-organizing conferences with me.

Thank you to Andrew Folco and Kim Reany for helping me process so much paperwork for events.

Thank you to Kari Kuo for your edits, Amber Berson for sharing your resources on childcare, and Kit Chokly for sharing your guide to cleaning transcripts.

Thank you to Ryan Van Huijstee for always providing feedback and editorial support on my projects.

Thank you to Sprout, Bubbles, and Pierre who all supported me at different points in developing this manuscript.

No acknowledgement section could fully encapsulate my gratitude for the people and animals whose scholarship, art, activism, teaching, and ways of being in the world have inspired me. Thank you to everyone who made this book possible.

ADDITIONAL RESOURCES

For further reading, check out these free resources:

- *Design Justice: Community-Led Practices to Build the Worlds We Need* by Sasha Costanza-Chock (MIT Press, 2020) is available open access at: mitpress.mit.edu/books/design-justice

- Amber Berson and Juliana Driever's Let Down Reflex on childcare: www.projectspace-efanyc.org/the-let-down-reflex

- Nicole J. Georges' podcast *Sagittarian Matters,* episode from May 20, 2016, in which she interviews music manager Tara Perkins and has a great discussion around the politics of paying artists.

- The Accessible Campus Checklist for Planning Accessible Conferences has some useful tips: www.accessiblecampus.ca/wp-content/uploads/2016/12/A-Checklist-for-Planning-Accessible-Events-1.pdf

- Native Land Digital's maps and resources: native-land.ca

- For more on auto-captioning tools and delivering accessible presentations, see the work of Rua M. Williams: www.ruamae.com/disability-advocacy/delivering-accessible-presentations/.

- UK Home Office, "Designing Accessible Services," 2019, ukhomeoffice.github.io/ accessibility-posters/?fbclid=IwAR0sV9gdcby8fCB8Y9rKUiOUHOzhOFLc5wQIh-4AIBt-dXw R9kFR-Ew0Fga

- The Association of Registered Graphic Designers has a free, in-depth guide, *AccessAbility 2: A Practical Handbook on Accessible Graphic Design:* rgd.ca/working-in-design/resources/accessability-2-a-practical-handbook-on-accessible-graphic-design

- While it is outside of the scope of this book to explain grant applications in full, Beth Pickens and Betty S. Lai have created useful materials for grant writing.

- Joe Biel's *Make a Zine!* and *A People's Guide to Publishing* and Laura Portwood-Stacer's book *Proposal Book* are also super helpful resources on publishing after your conference wraps up.

About the Lands We Are On

Everything that we do is tied to the land. I wrote most of this book while living in Tiohtià:ke (Montréal) on unceded Kanien'kehà:ka territory. These lands and waterways have also been a homeland and gathering place for many, including the Wendat, Abenaki, and Anishinaabeg peoples. I am grateful to the stewards of the land and waters from which I eat and drink.

I also want to acknowledge the people of the many lands that hold the servers enabling my research and writing, and the minerals that formed my technological devices. I thank the Tongva and Kizh people of Southern California who are custodians of the lands on which I was born and raised. The publisher of this book, Microcosm is located in Portland, Oregon on the lands of the Multnomah, Wasco, Cowlitz, Kathlamet, Clackamas, Bands of Chinook, Tualatin, Kalapuya, Molalla, and other Indigenous peoples who made their homes along the Wimahl (Chinook) Nch'i-Wāna (Yakama)/swah'netk'qhu (Sinixt)/Columbia (English) River.

As this book seeks to draw attention to power relations that have been invisibilized, it is important to acknowledge both Canada's and the United States' long colonial histories and current political practices. Interwoven with this ongoing history of colonization is one of enslavement and racism. I wrote this book while employed by McGill University, a university whose namesake, James McGill, enslaved Black and Indigenous peoples. It was in part from the money he acquired through these violent acts that McGill University was founded.

These histories and continued injustices inform the conversations within this text. Let us strive for respectful relationships with all the peoples of this land so that we can work towards collective healing and true reconciliation.

ABOUT THE AUTHOR

*A*lex Ketchum, PhD is an Associate Professor of Gender, Sexuality, Feminist, and Social Justice Studies at McGill University and the Director of the Just Feminist Tech and Scholarship Lab. Ketchum has organized several conferences including the hybrid Queer Food Conference, the Food, Feminism, and Fermentation Conference, and the food, feminism and technology conference, *Circuits de consommation: Art, activisme et la biopolitique du contrôle alimentaire*. She organizes a yearly Feminist Research Colloquium and has organized hundreds of events, including lectures, battles of the bands, book readings, organic pumpkin festivals, workshops, and art shows.

Notably she has organized over 106 events for her SSHRC funded speaker series, Disrupting Disruptions: the Feminist and Accessible, Publishing, Communications, and Tech Speaker and Workshop Series (see free video recordings of events at DisruptingDisruptions.com). Ketchum is the author of several books including *Ingredients for Revolution: A History of American Feminist Restaurants, Cafes, and Coffeehouses* (2022) and *Engage in Public Scholarship! A Guidebook on Feminist and Accessible Communication* (2022). She is the co-editor of *Queers at the Table: An Illustrated Guide to Queer Food with Recipes* (2025). With Microcosm, she has published the zines *How to Start a Feminist Restaurant* (2018), *How to Organize Inclusive Events* (2020), and *How to Organize Inclusive Conferences* (2024).

A historian by training, Ketchum works to make queer and feminist history more accessible. For more information, visit AlexKetchum.ca.

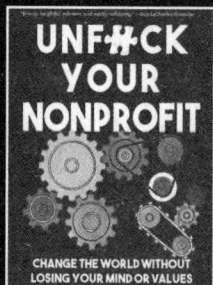